*I knew Arlene when she was very young. Her parents, Dave and Rowene were ministry acquaintances, committed, faithful, loyal, and passionate. Arlene was a pure, innocent, child - full of joy, hope, love, and faith. She had a gentle nature yet strong, uncompromising yet full of honor and sweetness ...and she sure loved her Lord.*

*When we first heard the news about Arlene being attacked with cancer, I wept deeply. How could this be as she was so young and full of purpose and destiny? We prayed fervently for her and received a great report soon after - the cancer had gone into remission. Over the next few years, however, we remained in the battle with rest periods in between reappearances of the disease.*

*When you read this book, you will be moved within. Arlene wrote most of it before she went to glory. It is written from her heart... from the meditations of a young girl filled with dreams... a young girl facing eternity. It will fill you with emotions that are hard to express. You will be touched as you enter her journey... I was.*

*Patricia King*
*Extreme Prophetic Ministries*

\*\*\*\*\*\*\*\*

i

"A Princess Meets Her Prince Charming" is the exceptionally touching story of the strong faith of a young girl battling for her life.

Arlene Sheppard, a missionary kid in Mexico, was a young teenager when she and her family were told she had leukemia. Thus began years of treatments and remissions, eventually ending in her passing to go home to the Lord.

During her short lifetime, Arlene touched many people's lives. Though her story is about her battle with cancer, the emotional ups and downs, and her strong faith throughout, it's also filled with deep love, commitment and joy. It is sure to touch your life in ways you wouldn't think possible.

Arlene's book takes you through her fight, beginning with the discovery of her cancer, climaxing with her Make A Wish Foundation visit with Prince Charles, in Buckingham Palace, back through another battle with leukemia and ending with a letter from Arlene's parents, missionaries David and Rowene Sheppard.

Even though Arlene is now in heaven, here is a touching story that deserves to be heard.

*Rick Osborne*
*Author: 101 Things Children Ask About God*

# A Princess Meets Her Prince Charming

**Author:** Arlene Joy Sheppard

**Participating authors and co-editors:**
**David, Rowene and Michael Sheppard**
d.sheppard@mail.com

# Contents:

# Dedication:

We dedicate this book with our love and appreciation to Vicky Love, an accomplished author and dear friend, who cheered Arlene along and gently made suggestions for improvements. We also will never forget the professional, compassionate care given to her by Dr. Moreno and the rest of the medical team.

Our thanks as well go to Ernita Beasley of Make-a-Wish UK and Brooke McAlister and the other volunteers at Make-a-Wish Yukon/ British Columbia who put together all of the details and arrangements to fulfill the wish of a lifetime.

We cannot forget to mention the kindness shown us by HRH Prince Charles for taking time out of his busy summer schedule to give a courageous girl and her family an unforgettable audience with him at Buckingham Palace. Without this exciting happening this book would lack much of its charm.

Last but not least, we sincerely thank the hundreds of friends, our parents and family members, who prayed with us through every crisis and supported us with love, letters, and finances. To God be all the glory for giving us strength, hope, grace and comfort in every moment.

# Prologue

I remember that in March 1997, David, Rowene, and Arlene came to my office. Another pediatrician who suspected Arlene to have a type of Hematological disease had sent them to me. After asking them some questions, and hearing about some of the symptoms, like osteo pain in the ribs, spine, and extremities, red dots (petechia) and bruises (ecchymosis), I pretty much knew what it was. Other children in these same circumstances often have repetitive infections, fevers with no apparent reason, nosebleeds, and bleeding gums. As I checked Arlene over, I noticed that she was pale, had petequias on her thorax and extremities, swollen glands (adenomegalias) on her neck, and under her arms (maxillary and axillary), as well as a swollen spleen. With this knowledge, and with the blood test they had brought, I told them about the high possibility that Arlene had leukemia and that we would have to take special tests to confirm or to rule out the possibility. One of the tests required the puncturing of the hipbone to aspirate a sample of the bone marrow and another to obtain cephalorrhachidian liquid—this is where Arlene's "piquetes" (needles) began.

Once we had received the results of the tests, it was confirmed that Arlene had Common Acute Lymphoblast Leukemia type B. Like Arlene says in one of her paragraphs: "A few years ago, those very words were definite death sentences to many people, especially children. " Fortunately, now days, because of the many medical advances in the diagnoses of and of the treating medicines, children with cancer can be cured.

When I told Arlene's parents the news, David told me that God was going to help Arlene. I responded that we couldn't just leave all of the work to God, but that we, too, had to work. So, David, Rowene, Arlene, and I formed a team to combat the disease with treatments based on the medicines (chemotherapy).

So, in the month of April, we set off on this new adventure. The first stage (Induction phase and prophylaxes to the Central Nervous system), is very important as we have to gain control of the disease. The 8 of May of 1997, we performed tests and received our first bit of good news—"Arlene is in remission" (there wasn't any sign of leukemia in her body, nor in her laboratory results).

The 26 of May of 1997, Arlene was hospitalized to begin one of the most complicated and dangerous phases of the treatment (Consolidation Phase). High doses of chemotherapy are given causing the red cells (hemoglobin), white cells (leucocytes), and platelets to be greatly lowered. This all can cause infections and massive bleeding, therefore putting the life of the patient in danger.

This phase was one of the most difficult for Arlene, her parents, grandparents, and me, as she got an infection (Sepsis) and had massive bleeding. Believe me that one day we couldn't control the bleeding and I thought that we would lose her. But thanks to God and our human team, Arlene got out of the hospital.

During this time, we had to take out the port that had been put in before the Consolidation period. We then continued on with the Maintenance Phase of the treatment. This stage consisted of Arlene having treatment every 6 weeks, and thankfully we had no more complications. However, Arlene was the one who had to receive all of the "piquetes".

As I mentioned in the lines before, thanks to the team (I only say team, because God formed part of it), we made it to the "far away" goal. The 27 of October 1999, the last chemotherapy treatment was given!

It has now been 3 years since Arlene finished her treatment and she is completely healed. Every 12 months, I have a check-up with her to make sure everything is well. Fortunately, Arlene comes to my office not only as a patient, but also as a friend!

Thank you, Arlene, for letting me be your doctor and friend!

And remember: "NEVER GIVE UP HOPE!"

Dr. Arturo Moreno Ramírez
Pediatric Onco-Hematologist
Ex-President of Oncology in Mexico


Translation done by Arlene Sheppard

**Dr. Moreno and Arlene**

# "You"

*"When I cry, You come to comfort me.*

*When I am bored, You come and make me giggle.*

*When I look at nature, You make it seem brighter.*

*When I cry, You wipe away my tears.*

*When I contemplate You, You blow my mind...*

*At Heaven's gate, You come and welcome me with open arms..."*

Written by Arlene Sheppard 1999
" And lo, I am with you always..."

# Chapter One—

# "You have Cancer."

One moment the sun may shine brightly and everything may look fun and exciting and hopeful—until a cloud temporarily blocks the sun and a shadow seems to hover over your life. One day, a cloud came, like a thief in the night, to try and steal my joy and hope, but I would not let it. That cloud was leukemia.

--------

The warm, spring sun penetrated through the windows as two teenage girls filled the room with laughter.

"Do you remember the time he wrote you that note?"

"Oh ya, that was great! What about the time our teacher yelled at us for coming to class late?"

"I know, I was so scared I was practically trembling..."

RING!!

"Just a minute," said Lisa as she went to answer the phone. "Hello, oh yes, Mr. Sheppard...Arlene?"

"Hey Dad, can I stay over at Lisa's house tonight? I'm on vacation now."

"I think you had better talk to your mom first..."

Disappointed, I hung up the phone, said good-bye to Lisa, and walked around the corner to the school to meet my parents. My dad was sitting in our van outside the school. My mom was inside the school's library getting a book to read over the Easter vacation. I made my way there to get a book at my mom's suggestion. In the back of the room, I looked at the series of books I was presently reading. Now, you must realize that I go to a small missionary school with an overloaded "petite" library. There were a couple of teachers in the room talking with my mom as she checked out her book. I overheard them mention something about leukemia. One of the teachers commented to my mom,

"You know, you should talk to Mrs. Morock. Her sister had that."

Questions and confusion began to flood my head. Once my mom and I joined my dad in the car, I was overwhelmed. With tears in my eyes I demanded,

"What's this all about?"

Then they uttered the worst news I had ever heard in my life.

"Arlene, the doctor called with the results of the bone marrow examination. He says that you have acute lymphoblastic leukemia."

--------

A few years ago, those very words were definite death sentences to many people, especially children. Of course, I did not know that then. However, the thought had never occurred to me that I could have cancer. I could not comprehend it. I was only fourteen years old. A lot of girls that age have a hard enough time coping with the physical and emotional changes in their bodies—big mountains indeed—but I had an Everest to get over. Pain and confusion came, but again, peace that surpasses any understanding just filled me so that I could know that " My grace is sufficient for you, for My strength is made perfect in weakness..." (II Corinthians 12:9). Little did I know that I would test and prove that verse to a deep degree....

--------

My parents planned for us to have a fun weekend before being checked into the hospital on Monday. It was Good Friday. We went to Pizza Hut, where I immediately headed for the bathroom to finish crying while my parents ordered the pizza. Then, we rented a video and drove home. On Easter Sunday, we had a special dinner at the house of some missionary friends, the Loves. After being loved on by the Loves, we arrived home and packed for the hospital. This was to be my first trip to the hospital since the day I was born.

--------

I feel I must recap my experience of the bone marrow examination that led to all these events. You see, several months before all of this, I had started having pain in my ribs. When I laughed — which is something I do all the time! — they would ache. Then that went away and I began having pain in my back. My mom took me to see the doctor next door and he declared it to be "nothing systemic" and told me to go see a chiropractor. When I went to see the chiropractor, he declared that I had scoliosis. However, we found the chiropractor expensive and useless for my needs.

We then went to a physiotherapist who gave me exercises to do, and different massages that were supposed to help ease the pain. The massages, again, were also of little use, because we were only treating the symptoms and not the root cause. My back hurt so badly at times that I could hardly walk. I would slither off my bed slowly and gently get up and walk to the bathroom grabbing hold of things on my way there.

Finally, I was taken to an orthopedic surgeon who declared I had fibromyalgia, a syndrome that basically says you can no longer do any type of physical activity for the rest of your life, or so the doctor told me. I had all the symptoms of fibromyalgia — pain everywhere — but the fact that I was as pale as a sheet did not fit. I also had incredibly large bruises on my arms, which had an inexplicable origin and lasted for weeks. Little red dots had appeared on my legs as well. Being suspicious of the anemia and my condition, the orthopedic surgeon had us set up an appointment with a renowned hematologist for several weeks later. If we had waited that long, possibly there would have been no need for an appointment....Acute leukemia, if not treated, can bring death to a person within a short period of time.

One day, I was too ill to attend school; I had an ear infection and was extremely weak, so I stayed home. After awaking, my mom announced to me that she had called a lab technician to come and take a blood test and urine sample. I screamed with the simple test, and the man looked at my watered down, sickly blood with a worried expression. We were given the results that night. My blood levels were alarmingly low, and strange cells called blastos, had multiplied to mass quantity in my blood. My mom called several doctor friends and they were all alarmed. I was taken to my pediatrician, who said I might have some kind of blood disease like aplastic anemia. He recommended that I see Dr. Arturo Moreno Ramírez, a pediatric onco-hematologist (children's blood and cancer specialist). Dr. Moreno, has been my doctor since then and his three specialties were perfect for my need. The Lord knew what was going on and had everything under control...

The night of my visit, Dr. Moreno looked at the red dots on my legs, called petechia, noted my enlarged spleen, read the blood test results, and was quite sure I had leukemia. The only way to be sure of it was to jab this dreadfully large needle into my back hipbone, puncturing it, and then sucking up a sample of the bone marrow. I had no idea how painful this would be, because the word "piquete" in Spanish (only a small prick) gave me the impression of something small and not too painful. Little or not, I hated needles and was terrified of them. When the time came for the sample to be taken, I experienced the worst pain I had ever felt in my life. My screams pierced the clinic and tears of anguish flowed hot on my cheeks. I remember going home so sore that it felt like I was still having the test. My brother, Michael, moved by my tears, sweetly planted a kiss on my forehead. I thought I would never ever have to have a bone marrow test again in my life.... Little did I know what was ahead.

--------

Interestingly enough, though I was so anemic, to the point that my normally rosy cheeks were white, and I would get terribly out of breath just going up the stairs at my school, I kept on with life in full force. People at my school would ask me if I was feeling OK since I was so pale, and I would respond, "I feel fine." I would go home crying, because I did not know why I was so pale. Since my back was so sore, I could not go to physical education because anything I did would cause agony. I could not even sneeze without it hurting terribly. However, despite having a hemoglobin count of 6, I managed to keep playing the flute. In fact, when I was diagnosed with leukemia, I was preparing for a concert that never did happen. I was in the eighth grade and decided to participate in the school spelling bee, just for the fun of it without studying. I actually won and went to Mexico City to compete there in the National Championship Spelling Bee. With what little energy I had, we raced through the massive subway system to get to the place of competition on time. It is amazing I could do all this. God is amazing!

The journey into treatment was going to be difficult and very painful, but I knew I would make it with God's help. The cloud of leukemia was dark and dense, but I felt I had hope, a bright Son shining, who was extending His light over me. The showers of trials might soak me, but God's promise with the rainbow would come.

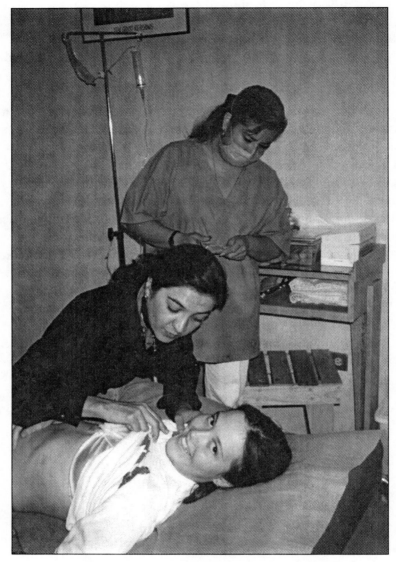

**AJ with Surgeon preparing to insert a cathetor**

# Chapter 2 —

# "And the Mountain Climbing Begins..."

*"I thought I'd write a few lines as my children have. They send much love over the miles. Cherysh sent crayons, because she thought you (Arlene) might like to color her picture. She kept adding things to her card and confessed that she couldn't quit, because her heart wanted to send you comfort. Destyni told me that the other night she woke up and was praying to the Lord for Arlene and was crying. She didn't know if that was okay (to be crying while you pray). I explained to her that it was more than all right. It was called crying out to God, because her prayer was so very sincere and heartfelt. My wee ones are learning much through this trial as we all are.... There is much prayer and petitioning going on on your family's behalf.*

*I am quite at a loss for words—on a human level, I wish we could pack into mom and dad's luggage and be there for support—on a spiritual level I know we're doing what is more important, and that's having faith that the Lord's will be done—we can not faint nor lose faith.*

*We are behind your family in much prayer—know this. We send hugs and kisses galore. Xoxoxo Lee-Ann, Bob, Destyni, Cherysh, and Tresyre. (My aunt and uncle and cousins.)"*

--------

*" Leukemia. Cancer of the blood. Don't have fibromyalgia after all. Yeah! But something that I hate with my whole being, leukemia. Monday, March 31, I go to the hospital to get more tests. But last night I had the most painful test, a needle in my hipbone to get bone marrow. It was a terrible experience! How can I express the grief leukemia has put on me today? But the Lord is going to make me happy again. Amen! I just can't believe it! Why me? Leukemia? Why? The Lord is going to help me through this difficult challenge in my life.*

*Tutu and Bapa* (my grandparents from Canada) *are arriving Tuesday, April 1, but I can't go to get them cause I'll be in the hospital! Bu-hu! I wanted to pick them up. I wanted to go see them. And when they see me, I'll be in the hospital! How depressing. But I'm not going to get depressed! In Jesus' name, give me extra happiness! Tutu and Bapa don't know yet (that I have leukemia), neither does Michael* (my brother). *They'll find out soon enough, though. Poor them! It will be hard on them also... Lord help me! I need extra strength, patience, love, and peace for this awful time! And Healing! Amen!" (Diary #1, March 27, 1997).*

--------

I walk into the hospital, a slight shiver making its way down my spine, as I look around in terror of the unknown. They take me to my room, which is a lot nicer than I expected. At first we enter a sort of "waiting room" (waiting for what?!). A strange picture hangs on the cream colored walls. Foam chairs are situated around the room. Then we stroll through this large similarly painted door, into what was to be my sleeping quarters. I gingerly sit on the single bed in the middle of the room to avoid any sudden, extreme pain in my back. I notice with delight that my bed can go up and down! A brown cot lies next to the window for my mom to sleep on. From where I sit, I can see through my window. *Hmmm.... the blue sky looks cheery enough, and those old, run-down buildings could provide interesting entertainment. Is that a black and white cat I see?* In front of me is a small TV, so that is nice. To my right, is a large marble sink and another big door to the bathroom. Having my own room is a plus. However, my nightmare day was just about to start...another cloud was coming...

"Arlene, they want to take a blood test," said Mom. "Oh, Mom, not another one!"

As the test was being taken, tears filled my eyes. That was nothing compared to what happened next....

"¡Hola Arlene!" says Doctor Moreno as he parades into the room carrying high the largest needle I have ever seen. Another bone marrow test is going to be taken. *I cannot believe it! I thought I would never have to have one again in my life and this is two in one week!* I lie face down on my bed as he began to clean the area and feel for the right place to jab the needle. Terrible fear and anxiety fill my mind as the precious seconds tick by. Then,

"AHHHHHHHHHHHHHHHHHHHHHHHHH! It hurts, Mommy, it hurts!! AHHHHHHHHHHH! Is he almost done yet?!!!"

reverberates throughout the area. Having finished his "dirty work," Doctor Moreno takes his leave. I lie exhausted from the exertion of it all, when breakfast is brought in. Skeptically, I examine it. *Hmmm...quesadillas... not too bad.* Then a man walks in pushing a wheelchair.

"Umm, I'm supposed to take Arlene downstairs for X-rays."

*There goes my possibility of recuperating somewhat with a hot breakfast. The wheelchair is cool. I have never been in one before; this could be fun.* Once down in the X-ray room, I lie on this narrow, cold table following the orders:

"Ok, Arlene, don't breathe...Now you can relax...Don't move... here goes another one..."

And on and on it went until all ten head to foot X-rays were taken. I have never had so many before. Upon arriving back to my room, I attempt to eat the cold breakfast. A little later, a nurse steps into my room, and I think, " Now what?!" She wants to start an IV. In goes needle number one into my right arm, dig, dig, dig. *Oh, God, when is it going to be over!* Pain is wrenching my body, causing havoc to break out in my brain. I want to move, to get away from it all.

"Don't move, Arlene, you'll knock the needle out of place."
"Relax, if you don't, we can't get it in."

*Great, blaming me in a situation that is not my fault. Why is it always my fault it doesn't get in?* She then pulls the needle out; that vein is not going to work. She could not find it. *Oh good, temporary relief.* She decides to try in my other arm. *Ok, put my arm down to get the veins to pop out more. Ouch, that tourniquet pulls my skin! That alcohol swab is cold! Yikes, that needle hurts! Oh great, here she goes again, digging and digging. Why can't she just hurry up and get it in?* She takes it out again and leaves the room. I lie there once again out of breath.

"Hey mom, why can't she get it in?"
"I don't know. Maybe it's because you're so anemic. Anemia sometimes makes your veins appear to hide, making it difficult to locate one."
"Mom,"
"Yes, Lovey?"
"I don't want another one. It hurts too much."
"I know. I wish I could take it for you. My veins are so obvious, compared to your pretty little ones."

The nurse returns, this time with a guy with her. *Please no! Tell me it's not necessary!* He looks at my arms and declares that I have good veins and shoves the needle in one on the first try. *Oh, he is good. Yes, it hurt, but at least it was quick! I am sure glad that is over with. Praise the Lord! I can now rest. Whew, what a day!*

--------

I made it through the cloud. I made it over that mountain. The day was not all-bad. My friend Anna came and brought me some flowers and a cute book and her cheerfulness. Later we got the results from all the tests, and knew how bad the leukemia was. My white cells were 60% cancerous. Many of my bones were badly eaten away by the disease, causing the pain in my back.. I would soon be starting chemotherapy.

# Chapter 3—

# " The Good, the Bad, and the Downright Ugly."

"Dear Arlene.

Hi! Hope you're recuperating well. I feel really badly, because your gums were bleeding and you had to go back to the hospital. You must have been happier to get out, but sad to go back in...."

--------

O nce again, I was faced with the unknown. I was having new experiences all of the time! Chemotherapy was just another one, right? It couldn't be as bad as rumors say or could it? People lose their hair and spend every last bit of their energy throwing up their dinner. Then, they pass out. Hollow faces with suffering eyes, bald heads, and skin-bone bodies. Could this be? Do these Kool-aid colored " poisons" really do that to you?

### Chemo—What in the World is that?!!!

Basically, chemotherapy is just that—chemicals given as a therapy. It kills the bad, cancerous cells in a person's body, but also kills the good ones, like hair and skin cells. Since these are weaker, they are usually the first to go—which is why people lose their hair and have sensitive skin after their chemo treatments. Often it causes you to have a sore mouth, because the cells of the mucous membrane are affected. If the right medications aren't given to prevent some of the action of the chemo, a person can get bad ulcers in their digestive tract.

Some of the drugs are so strong that they can damage the heart, which is why you must be closely monitored while taking them. (Only people with cancer or other diseases should take them.) Chemo is overall dangerous and bad for you, but to state it bluntly, medically speaking, it is your choice either to suffer through chemotherapy and its affects or die of cancer.

### The Protocol for my type of leukemia

As I mentioned earlier, if acute leukemia is not found and treated, a person can die in weeks. You must get the leukemia into remission within 6-8 weeks. We rather misunderstood the doctor, and thought that after the 6 weeks of chemo, my treatment would be over. Little did I know at the time that my protocol was to last for more than 2 and a half years.

### And the Chemo begins...

At the beginning of my treatments, I was going every day for chemo at a clinic. The chemicals often irritated the area of skin around the I.V., caused me to have bad headaches and sometimes, nausea. I had a lot of these affects, especially at the beginning of the treatment, as I was having so much of it and my body was not at all used to it yet.

The month of April went by in a hurried frenzy of chemotherapy. *"I've had Chemo six days a week for two weeks. Several of those painful back medication shots too. I had a two and a half hour surgery to get a catheter* (port) *put in, so they don't have to find a vein every day they want to give my Chemo. Wow! So much has happened! But the Lord is going to heal me! Amen. In a way I can say, that I have found a way to be grateful for this terrible experience. This sounds weird, but I'm growing spiritually with this experience and I know*

*God is going to heal me and is doing it right now. I no longer have leukemia cells (cancer cells) in me! (And am now in remission.) Hallelujah! And my blood is getting better all the time! Yes! I guess I'm like Job, in the Bible, all these terrible things happened to him, but God knew he could make it and become a better person. So, I guess He's doing that with me, because He knew that I could do it. Also, maybe then, I can help and comfort others in a special way..."* (Diary #1, Month of April, 1997).

I was introduced to another very painful backshot. This injection required putting in a rather large needle into my spine, between the vertebrae, aspirating a sample of spinal fluid in order to check it, and then injecting some chemo into my spine. I had to sit cross-legged on the bed with my head tucked down so that my spine could be exposed. Dr. Moreno would then have to feel around in the lower part to see where he was to put the needle. My nurse would then pass him the cleaning solutions on a gauze and he would clean it, pressing quite firmly into the spine. (YUCK!!! I get the hibbi-gibbies just writing this!!) Then the needle process would begin. When the chemo was injected, all the nerves up and down my legs would hurt and scream out. Then it was over. The whole process lasted about 5 minutes, but the most agonizing 5 minutes. After the backshot, I was to lie flat for a while and was encouraged to shake my legs a bit to spread the medication throughout my nerve endings to help with the remaining ache. These injections brought on headaches, which would sometimes stay in the background for days and sometimes weeks.

During this period, I went through various stages of treatment. After I got into remission, I entered a stage called " consolidation". This stage was the most difficult of all. Instead of having a bone marrow transplant, I was basically killed off with intensive chemotherapy and then brought back to life with these injections that stimulated my bone marrow to reproduce blood cells once again. I endured 24 hours of chemo drip for 5 days, then I would go home for the weekend, and come back for another 5 days of 24-hour drip. My blood count dropped to the zero range. It was practically like water as it didn't have much "blood" substance. I should have been put into complete isolation, but I wasn't until it was almost too late...

## The Fever

"Roses are Red, Violets are blue,
Oh, how I want to see you up
*and running too!"*

*"Dear Arlene, I just wanted to write you a little note to cheer you up. I hope you feel better very soon. I have been praying for you. I want to see you up and normal again.... I love you a lot and hope your temperature goes way down. Love Harmony."*

During this time, I got E. Coli. This infection caused a fever of 42° C (104° F). For two weeks it burned in my body. I had diarrhea until I could go no more. My hemoglobin (red cells) was down to 2; so low that I didn't have the strength to even get up. My platelets were at a dangerous level of 10, 000 and below. I slept and slept. Nurses, as well as my mom and grandmother, bathed my body with ice-cold cloths to try to break the fever. I would lie in shivering agony for hours. I wasn't allowed any more than a sheet on my "cold" body.

Pastors would come to pray for me. My church in McAllen, Texas, fasted and prayed for me for 7 days. My church here in Puebla, Mexico, did it for 4. The Lord protected me so much. I could have gone into delirium, but I never did. I could have died, for that matter, but the thought never even entered my mind. God had other plans for me.

Mom had to exercise my muscles and joints for me by gently turning my ankles and arms round and round. However, I ended up losing most of my muscles anyway. When the time came for me to leave the hospital, I couldn't stand up by myself. My grand-mother and mother had to stand on either side of me to hold me up. I couldn't walk. I had to re-learn to walk at the age of 14. Slowly but surely my strength was regained. Praise the Lord!

We found out that there was some E. Coli in my port. Since, my blood in my veins had gone down so low, the skin over the port opened up, leaving an oozing sore. Naturally, as the port is connected directly to the jugular and can take the infection straight to the heart, killing you, we had to take it out. However, they couldn't operate on me until my blood level was better. So, every day my wound had to be cleaned and every time it was a tortuous experience. I didn't want to be put asleep again during the surgery because I didn't want to have to have another IV started, so they just froze the area. Even though I couldn't feel pain, I could feel this tugging just below my right shoulder. I can still remember hearing the "snip-snip" of the scissors as they cut away the worn out, damaged skin. Once again, I was saved from possible death.

--------

After surviving this crisis time, I entered a stage called "maintenance". During this phase, I was hospitalized for chemotherapy every 6 weeks for a little over a year and a half. They gave me an "ABC" treatment. This basically meant that one time I would have the red chemo, which would require two afternoons in the clinic and a backshot; another was a clear liquid that called for a 24-hour hospital stay and a backshot; and finally, a yellow one—the longest hospital bout: 24-hours of chemotherapy and then 3 days of "rescue" injections every 6 hours to counteract the affects of the killer medications as well as another backshot. And then there was the bone marrow exam every 3 months. Between chemo I.V.'s, I was constantly on oral medication. The week following the I.V., I had to take Meticortin, cortisone pills.

The last stage of all, is the one that I'm on right now—vigilance. I go in for a blood test, bone marrow, and spinal tap every three months for a year. After that, it's every six months for another year.

In truth, I went through many storms during the different stages of my protocol, but "Praise God who gives us (me) the victory!" (From 2 Corinthians 2:14)

--------

## What a Pain!

*Throughout most of my treatments, I often suffered with cramps in my calves, especially right after having that fever and all the chemotherapy just before it. When I lay in the hospital bed, I was scared to even bend my toes, as they would cramp in a nasty way and hurt. Eventually, that went away, but for many months, practically every night I would wake up in the middle of the night with horrible cramps in my legs that I would have to rub and rub and pray hard for them to go away. Many times, the pain caused me to cry out in agony. Thankfully, I hardly ever have that anymore! Praise the Lord!*

*Some of the medications also caused my bones in my legs to ache. For about a year after "The Fever" I would begin to have pain in my knee area also, about one week before I was to take the Meticortin steroid pills again. The Meticortin was good at taking away pain, and clearing up skin rashes from the chemo. By God's grace I'm now free from that too!*

*Jesus, my ultimate physician, specializes in repairing and restoring that which was damaged— completely, and that's what He did in me!*

# Chapter 4

# "Hair Today, Gone Tomorrow"
# (The Case of the Hairy Pillow)

*"I think you look very pretty with your wig!
I promise I like it. And it does not look funny
or stupid at all!... Love ya tons, Harmony"*

--------

## Catherine

*Most all of my treatments were done here in Mexico.
However, I was treated once in the Children's Hospital in
Vancouver, B.C.. That was a bit of a change. The food was
maybe a little better, the game room was great, but I had
never shared a hospital room before and I wasn't sure that I
wanted to.*

*At first, I had my own room, but when a kid came who
needed isolation, I was quickly moved, in the middle of the
night, to the room next door. I heard a horrible gagging and
coughing sound, that made my innards roll, too, coming
from the bathroom and thought, "Is this what it's gonna be
like with a roommate? How am I supposed to sleep?!" In
the morning, I awoke to 'Hello friends, it's Barney, you're
friendly dinosaur!' and thought, "Good grief! I also have to
put up with the kid's shows!" However, I found that despite*

*our age difference (she was ten, and I was 16), and after having to learn to put up with each other, we got along great! We'd paint and do crafts together in the playroom, decorate our bulletin board, share laughs and stories, and had at least one thing in common—we both had cancer. There we were having to push around our I.V.'s with the heavy pumps that beeped, eating not so good food, not feeling so well, and having our temperatures and blood pressure checked together! I found that I had a friend, not just a roommate and I loved her.*

*Once again, I had to learn to make the most of a situation. The Lord blessed and I actually had a good time in the hospital!*

--------

In the last chapter, I talked briefly about chemotherapy and its side affects. One of those affects is the loss of hair. Mine fell out eight different times. I would just be growing in a skiff of soft, furry hair and getting my eyelashes and eyebrows back, when I would have to take the red chemo again and lose them yet another time. It wasn't anything easy, especially in your teen years where looks are advertised and promoted as "every thing". Also, it didn't help to have a pale, puffy face.

The first time I lost my hair was, to say the least, one of the most difficult things that has ever happened to me. Chemotherapy affects people in different ways. Some people lose their hair every time they are subject to even light chemo, others with only certain kinds, and yet there are others who never lose it. I didn't lose mine until a good month after starting chemo. I had just taken the red chemo and was almost ready to be declared in remission. I still had my long, brown, silky, straight locks. We went to Acapulco beach for a vacation. In my hotel room, brushing my hair, I began to notice more than the usual amount of hair coming out. However, I was able to get my hair braided and didn't have to really think about the possibility of losing it for a while. Even when I returned, my doctor and nurse figured I wouldn't lose it as I hadn't lost it yet. I was really excited about that news. I wore the braids for the next two weeks before having to take them out.... I happened to be ending the fun of a slumber party with only two of my friends, Harmony and Amy, remaining. I asked them to help me take out the braids. I didn't realize that this day would be the last in years that I would have long hair...

Amy and Harmony worked hard at taking the braids out. I just sat there chatting and enjoying myself, while they let agony fly by.

" *Look at all this hair coming out, Harmony. Should I just let the wind take it?* " whispered Amy.
" *I guess so. I don't know what else to do.*"

An hour or so later,

*"Amy, can I borrow your hair-dryer? I don't want to go to the store with my bangs kinky."* I said.

As I wrapped some hair around the round brush, the clump of hair just came out!

*"Amy, look!! NOOOO! Now I have a bald spot right on my forehead!! What am I to do?"*

I rather lost my appetite for going to the candy store and called to have my dad pick me up. Later, as the shower water fell down my back, I screamed out, " *Mom, can you help me, please?!*" My hair was coming out in mass quantities. I was scared. I was sad. It all happened so fast. My mom tried desperately to comb the rest of hair down my back. She applied gobs and gobs of conditioner and worked for a long time de-tangling it. Eventually, only a few strands remained actually attached to my head with a ball of hair, like a rat's nest, hanging on to its ends. The sensation of the wet, matted hair on my back caused my back to itch. I could no longer stand it. *"Mom, cut it off!!"* I begged. Gently, she took some scissors and cut off what was left, to chin level. We called a neighbor hairdresser to see if she could make it look better. I was bald! That day was Mother's Day in Mexico. The next day was Sunday.

*" I took a shower and had to cut off my hair, what's left of it. I lost my hair! I'm almost completely bald. Why me? I guess I'll have an even stronger ministry now. I called Anna and she was really sad. I cried a lot and so did mom. I guess that's not a nice Mother's Day gift, huh? I look ugly! My face is fat from the Metacortin and my head is baldish! Oh well. The Lord is my strength. We're going to get a nice wig. But a wig's a wig. You can still tell it's not real. The guys in my class are really gonna make fun of me now especially..."* (Diary #1, May 10, 1997).

That day like I said was hard. However, the Lord knows how to perk you up.

*" Hey! good news! They got the results from the bone marrow and I'm now in official remission of leukemia! Yeh! Glory to God! That is really good. I still have affects of the chemo and still have to take it. I get headaches and my gums are really sore. But at least I don't vomit. Thank you Lord!* (Diary #1, May 10, 1997).

On Sunday, I wore a hat to church and was very teary-eyed. My pastor's daughter gave me a nice hat and my friends tried to cheer me up and protect me from criticism. One girl, looked at my thin, short strands of hair and asked, "Why did you cut your hair? It was so beautiful before!" Not knowing how to reply, my friends quickly came to my rescue, " She looks nice like this too." When something like this happens, you feel like everyone is already looking at you weird. It's nice to have friends who are with you even if you look horrible.

--------

Like I mentioned earlier, I would get very bored being in my room all the time, so to pass the time and to get a little exercise, when I was feeling up to it, we went for walks either down the halls or downstairs in the garden. I would usually cover my baldness with some sort of hat as I was embarrassed to have people see me like that. Eventually, I got to the point where I would walk around bald in the hospital. I couldn't care less. Sure, I got some stares of bewilderment and others of compassion, but I couldn't be bothered to put on a hot hat. I decided to go "au naturale". However, it took a long time for me to be able to get used to being bald around others.

As I said before, I lost my hair eight different times. Each and every time was heart-wrenching for my family and me. We got very used to my baldness and exuberant whenever I could go around with my short hair that was so soft. Sometimes I would even forget that I was "follicle impaired." One time at a school camp, I walked out of the cabin hatless to empty trash and then remembered my state and quickly went back inside. I actually got to the point that it seemed weird that other people had hair, had to wash it, and take care of it. I just had to slip on my wig and style it really fast. Often, some of my friends would complain about having a bad hair day or how horrible their new haircut was and I would think, *"Well, at least you've got hair!!"* I would look at their lovely, long eyelashes and wish for the day that mine would be like theirs. They also didn't have to paint their eyebrows to fill in sparse spots.

I still suffered judgment from people who didn't know me. One time I remember I was out swimming in a pool, bald and beautiful. I was talking to a girl when her little brother came over to us and asked, *"Why would any women shave her hair?!"* I answered with, *"I didn't shave it; I lost it."* The girl then asked, *"Cancer?"* and I responded, *"Yes."* If I wasn't worried about looking how I did, neither should he. Unfortunately, it doesn't seem to work out that way. Many people are born naturally curious and sometimes insensitive to the feelings of others. Because of this, many people suffer. It hurt me.

I often wondered if guys were scared of me; that they didn't know how to treat a bald girl. It made me feel bad. My friends and family were gracious to me and treated me well. I discovered that it is very important to have the support of the people close to you. If I were to advise people as to how to treat a person going through some terminal disease, it would be just show your support, love, and prayers for the person. Make them feel special. Don't treat them badly; they already have a difficult enough life. If they look kind of funny, you don't have to tell them that. Instead, compliment them on something else.

--------

*"I didn't wear my hat to church, and lots of people commented on how pretty I looked. I liked it. One guy said I looked like a model. A lady told me my face looked like a bouquet of roses"*(Diary#1,Sept 14, 2001).

Such comments always made me feel good, and I think that it is much better for the person, both emotionally and physically, to be happy with him or herself and have the assurance that the people around them approve of them as well.

--------

*"My hair has started falling out. Oh, Lord, why? Sometimes, I want to tell people that they don't know what it's like. They say 'I'm sorry' or 'It'll be OK', but they don't know what it's like. I guess they don't know what to say"* (Diary#2, January 30, 1998).

This is a very typical response that people give in this type of situation. I know that they are just trying to let you know that they support you, but if they really don't know what it is like, I suggest that it is better to try to say something else. If you are going through this and someone asks you, "What is it like to lose you hair?" Instead of shouting out, "Dreadful, ok!? Leave me alone!" you could perhaps take the view of my friend, Harmony, who once told me,

*"I'm sorry you're losing your hair again, but it'll grow back. At least, it's not like losing an arm or a leg."*

Though losing one's hair might feel like the end of the world, it's not. We will always find someone who is suffering far more than us.

When you are presented with difficult circumstances in your life, a lot of times the best thing you can do is to laugh it off. "Laughter is good like a medicine"(Proverbs 17:22). One time in particular, my cousin Morgan and I did just that. We wrote this short description to do just that—make us laugh off the pain. I had grown in some hair, but it had just started to fall out again....

*"...A lady came up to us and told me how beautiful my hair looked and how I should leave it. She then touched it! .... Meanwhile back at the ranch of Arlene's scalp, the hair follicles screamed, 'No don't touch me!' and slowly fluttered down to the resting place of the dearly departed hair among the shady shoulder blades.... The Lady made a small bald spot which Michael had to carefully conceal with the neighboring of the dearly departed. In the little girl's room (restroom), mom was mourning over the loss of the dearly departed. And I, noticing a stall was occupied, quickly indicated that it was time to hush" (Diary#3, June7, 1998— Morgan/Arlene productions).*

--------

Losing hair hurt not only emotionally, but physically as well.

*"I noticed today I have those red bumps on my head that I get from the red chemo. I don't think I normally get them from the chemos. Someone told me that when I get those on my head, that it's hair follicles exploding, pushing out hair"* *(Diary#5, Sept.30,1999).*

Those red bumps itched like horrible mosquito bites, but hurt when you scratched them. I also couldn't scratch them too much, as then I would get scabs. They were pesky little things.

The actual process of losing my hair was one of the most difficult things. Every morning, I would wake up with my pillow covered with hairs. It made just breathing most uncomfortable and annoying. I would try not to wash my hair until I had so many bald spots, that it no longer mattered. When I finally washed it, endless amounts of hair would come out. Sometimes they would even block the drain. I didn't like people seeing me in the half- hair/ half- bald stage. I found it more embarrassing then, as it looked like I had mange or something; it was pretty bad. I would tend to lose the hair around the sides of my head first, as that is where you lie on your pillow and where your shirts rub against when you're dressing. Eventually, I would just have a small patch on the top of my head. This is when my brother would call me "Moe," short for Mohawk. I could easily pull out hair; all you had to do was brush against it with your fingers or give a slight tug and you'd end up with these tiny curly hairs in your hands. In fact, as I would spend hours doing math homework, I literally pulled my hair out trying to do it. Ha-ha. One time, I even went to school as the King of Siam with my friend, Jenyne, as Anna for a dress-up Christmas party of famous couples of the 19th century. Mom put makeup on my head to make it the same shade as my face and neck (your head is quite white when you hardly ever expose it to the sun), and, though it got a few stares, especially from the little kids, I forced myself to stay calm and graceful in my part of the character. That's what you call making the most of a situation. Ha-ha

--------

The last time I lost my hair, we were at Puerto Vallarta for a vacation. We were celebrating the fact that I had finished all of my treatments. I was beginning to lose my hair again.

*"My hair has been falling out for several days now. However, it's now getting worse. It is horrible not to be able to swim with my head under the water, because it would leave a trail of hairs behind"*(Diary # 6, Nov. 15,1999).

Despite all of these hard trials, I remembered the verse, "Charm is deceitful and beauty is passing, but a woman who fears the Lord she shall be praised" (Proverbs 31:30, NKJV).

*"Though I'm bald, have extra short eyelashes, and few eyebrows left, I fear the Lord. I hope that shines through especially when my outside beauty doesn't that much"* (Diary # 1, Oct. 22, 1997).

This had to be my perspective in order to survive these years. I thank God that He is my help in time of present need, my refuge, my God in whom I trust (from Psalm 41:1 NKJV).

*" I was bored and sulking today, because it seems like I'm confined to the house or the hospital etc. I wanted to go and do something. Oh well. And also my eyelashes are so short 'cause they broke and my eyebrows are few and far between. I was thinking of what it would be like to have long hair again..."* (Diary #1 Oct. 25, 1997).

Somehow the Lord brought me through these trials as well. He is able. I now have been growing my hair for almost two years. It's glossy and curly! I'm always getting compliments for it and it's so much fun to once again have long hair! I praise God.

**Before – Michael and Arlene with long hair**

**Hair Today and gone tomorrow**

**Arlene with Daisy**

**Arlene with wig and sunglasses**

# Chapter 5

# "Life with Chemo"

### "Emergency"

"Here we are again, Dear Ones, in need of prayer —how valuable a resource. Last evening, Arlene was found to be in URGENT need of blood platelets and red blood cells. She is in a deep crisis. We are going to give blood platelets this morning. Please pray for Arlene as her platelets were at 16,000 yesterday and lower last night as well as her red blood count. Thanks David Sheppard "

### "Don't Panic—It is Well"

"Dear David and Rowene and Arlene,

This morning as I was praying for you, God showed me a picture of Arlene nursing her little baby and Jesus had His hand on her shoulder. It is a picture of joy and I could cry again as I am typing this note to you. Praise the Lord. "

--------

## An Awesome Miracle

*It was time for my treatments again and I went in for my blood test. The results showed that it was too low to have more chemotherapy administered. Dr. Moreno told me to go home, get the blood count up, and come back in a week.*

*So, the next day—the day I had been scheduled to have my treatment—I went over to my friend Harmony's house. She and I had had an enjoyable morning, playing games, telling tales, and had just sat down on her bouncy bed to continue doing so. Her boxer dog sat down on the bed and made it move up and down. Then, all of a sudden, the bed continued to shift back and forth and up and down. It hit us—we were experiencing an earthquake! It was quite strong and shook us until after we had run down the stairs and gone into the backyard. The deep rumble was strongly heard. A lot of damage happened in the city that day, especially in the downtown area, where my hospital is. Many of the old, Catholic churches had severe structural damage and even my hospital had its chapel in ruins. Scaffolding was up for years until everything was finally completely restored.*

*I could have been in the operating room that day, receiving my bone marrow and back shot. I could have been having an IV put in or any number of things, but the Lord protected me. He sure had His angels on the double that day!*

--------

My treatments consisted of Chemo, chemo and more chemo. It changed my lifestyle. Everything we did, everywhere we went, chemo affected us. We would have to plan our trips between hospital visits and doctor's appointments. It was involved in my daily life, forcing me to put up with nausea, headaches, and a sore mouth.

I remember one time in particular, when I felt so horrible that I could not eat at one of our favorite restaurants. At the time, I had a very large appetite from the Meticortin. However, the nausea was so bad that it took all I could do to keep from vomiting.

"Honey, would you like a taco?"

"No, mom, no...I can't...I...uh...don't feel well...please get that food away from me!"

"Are you sure?"

"Yes, you just go ahead and eat."

I had a splitting headache, too. I just lay my head on the table, while the smell of food surrounded me. When I got home, I went straight to sleep, as I couldn't hold off the nausea any longer. There were many other times that this happened to me as well. Often, I had wrenching headaches and had to take medication for it. Once a week, I would receive a dreaded backshot into my spinal fluid, to prevent cancer cells from infiltrating my brain and central nervous system. These would also cause more headaches.

Another time, I remember just having the red chemo and I was at school the next day, trying to make up for a test I had missed. I could no longer endure it; I was so terribly dizzy. I was forced to go home and take it another time.

The first time that I received the yellow chemo, I was watching TV when my throat started to close up. Dread filled me as I could hardly breathe or swallow. I had to remain calm though panic hit my body.

From both the yellow and red chemo I would get a really sore mouth. I would get big chancre sores all over in my mouth, especially around the entrance to my throat. There were times that I could hardly eat or drink, as the food would rub against my mouth and cause excruciating pain. I would have to gargle with baking soda water three times a day to clean my mouth and bring a little relief. However, one time, I gargled too often and it made it far worse—so sore that I could hardly talk. Other times, I couldn't sing well.

*" ...and my gums hurt so much that I can't sing! It's terrible because in a few days it's the spring concert at my school and I love to sing"* (Diary #1, May 12, 1997).

Just before I was officially declared to be in remission, I had taken the red chemo. My family and I were on vacation. We were at a restaurant eating, when all of a sudden, my hands started to twist and contort with cramps. It scared me! I didn't know what was happening to me. I was taken to a doctor, and he said the cause could be either from lack of potassium or from heavy chemotherapy. Well, I had been on high doses of chemotherapy. My hands bothered me for several days after and eventually got better.

At the beginning of my treatments, I was having high amounts of chemo. I had a backshot every week for six weeks and I guess it affected my nerves. My hands were slightly shaky. I found it difficult to write and even harder to paint my nails or do anything that calls for steady hands. I hated it. I couldn't keep my hands still. Thankfully, that, too, was only a passing phase.

During maintenance, I constantly had to take pills. I took about two little ones nightly and once a week over twenty pills in one night. When I had to take the twenty or so, I would swallow four or five of them at a time. After a while, the very thought of having to take those pills caused me to want to gag and sent shivers down my body. These pills caused me slight nausea and a sore mouth. So, I usually didn't feel optimum all of the time, as I would have these slight botherings. I hated having to take these pills wherever I went, even when I went camping with my school or stayed over at a friend's house. I couldn't just spontaneously stay somewhere as I had to make sure I had my pills. I am so thankful that I no longer have to live like that.

I also got tired quite often.

*"Today was the March for Jesus. I didn't go, because we figured that I probably couldn't make it.... I took a nap as my head was hurting and I had a busy morning. Man, it seems I'm always taking naps now and I use to not be able to"* (Diary#1, May 17, 1997). *" Today, I rested a lot...Very tired again. I forgot to take my pill last night, so when I awoke, I got scared. I was having problems breathing today, I hope that goes away..."* (Diary#1, May 19-20, 1997).

Chemotherapy was difficult not only for my body, but also for my mind. I would, as I mentioned earlier, gag at the thought of the pills. I also struggled deeply with fear of future "torture" sessions of the bone marrow and back shots, and with my appearance.

*"Oh, guess what? On Thursday, I might have another bone marrow test and the back test! Oh no! I wish they would put me to sleep, but I guess they won't. Oh well, no use in worrying about it now, the Lord will help"* (Diary#1, May 5, 1997).

*" I don't like to think about Thursday, but sometimes its hard not too. The Lord will help. Sometimes I still wonder, 'why me'? I didn't do anything wrong and I know that. That is not why I am having this trying time. But still, it is very difficult. Lord give me* peace, *joy, hope, happiness, strength, and, Lord, healing soon! Please! I love you! And I know You will help me!!"* (Diary#1, May 6, 1997).

-------

*"I'm not going to school tomorrow, only to music class I guess. So that might be a little easier. It's because of me being emotional, having aches and pains, etc. (I had just lost my hair) We looked for wigs, but found none. They were either ugly, old fashioned, the wrong color, or just not me! I look terrible!...Well, Lord, here I am. I need your strength, peace, love, joy, happiness, wisdom, etc. I need You! For I am nothing without You. Help my light to shine so bright that people won't even notice my outward appearance! Send me, help me, use me, here I am* (Diary#1, May11, 1997)! *"My hair doesn't fall out nearly as much anymore—that's good, but it looks like I might have more of the medication that made it fall out and gave me cramps in my hands and feet. Not nice"* (Diary #1, May 20, 1997).

--------

As I lay on the cot in the clinic watching the liquid drip down the tube, my heart, temperature, and blood pressure had to be checked periodically to ensure that no damage was taking place. (That my heart was handling the chemical onslaught OK.) After an hour or so of this, I would be disconnected from the I.V. and would go home and live a "normal" life. I would work hard to keep up with school and my music lessons.

When I went to the hospital, I would delightedly receive visitors. It was so boring in there; you could only watch TV for so long. I even made up a song to sing, when I was lonely for visitors. It went something like this,

*"When is anybody gonna visit me? Doctors, nurses with their BP. When is anybody gonna visit me?! Michael, daddy, anybody PLEASE, come and visit me!"*

Even though I enjoyed reading, I found it difficult to do; I had to fight off nausea and headaches. I also had only one hand to use to hold the book, as the IV hand would lie rigid to keep the IV in place. Visitors would occupy my thoughts and entertain me. They often brought me food that was actually "digestible" too. My friend, Anna, was good at "sneaking" in pizza, a food that I always seemed to be able to eat even if nauseated, and milkshakes.

I found my "Buddy ole pal" or my IV, a pain in the neck. Naturally, it was with me where ever I went. Mom and I would try to take walks around the hospital grounds, me walking and her pushing my post along with much difficulty. The stand that carried my IV was very unstable and the ground often uneven. There was also a heavy pump on it to regulate my chemo. This machine would "scrawble" or screech at any discomfort it had. Let me explain. If there was air in the tube, it would cry out; out of solution, it sure would let us know!; or out of battery, again it screamed in protest. The pump was no respecter of time either. It would make noise in the middle of the night just as easily as in broad daylight. It also ticked all of the time. This pump made it necessary for me to be connected to the wall most of the time, as the battery would run out. For some reason, the plug-in was always behind my bed, making it impossible for me to unplug it and whoever did would bang their hand against the wall pulling it out. My poor mother did this all too often. So, I even had to be escorted to the bathroom, have my few moments of privacy, and then have whoever was with me walk me out to the sink, where I attempted to wash my hands with only one hand.

Since I was going to be having a lot of IV's, they decided to put a little drum-port under my skin. This little gadget, that was to sit on my chest below my right shoulder, was to act as an easy-to-get-to vein. All the doctors would have to do is prick the skin over it into the port, and they could start the medication. I remember going to another hospital for the surgery. I had never been in an operation room before, and it was dark and scary. I didn't want to go in "alone"; the very nice surgeon allowed my mom in with me too. I lay there on the narrow table as the medics bustled about getting everything ready. Wrapping my long hair in a cloth like a turban and starting my IV were among the preparations. I nervously talked to mom as she tried to distract me from what was happening. A tear of anxiety escaped. We prayed for comfort, strength, and guidance for the doctor's hands during the surgery.... Suddenly, I woke out of oblivion to a horrible pain on my chest—they were putting a needle in the port, so not to be pricked later again when I went for more chemo. That afternoon, I painfully tried to rest. The stitches in my neck and on my chest stung and ached. I couldn't do anything but lay there crying and moaning. I had to have assistance getting up and lying down, as I didn't want the stitches to be pulled by using the muscles in my neck. Eventually, I got so that I was strong enough to hold my head on my own and could be normal again. I had to wear a big patch over it sometimes, which didn't look the greatest, nor did it give relief from the firm pressure of the port on my chest.

--------

Living with Chemo, meant having a lot of needles.

*"Needles are terribly painful things, but what I try to tell myself is it's a pain for a while, yes, but then it's sort of finished. I've had to go through a lot and still have more. I'm becoming a pincushion"* (Diary#1, May4, 1997).

One time that I remember not so fondly was the time that I lay for an hour and a half on the hospital bed, while they tried to get the IV started. I had my port at the time, and the doctor was trying to get a blood sample from it and then start the IV. I lay there miserable and in pain. A little blood was finally sucked up for the sample, but could not be used as it was diluted with heparin. So, again they would try, as I felt this painful sucking from my port. Eventually, they finally had to start an IV in my hand and get blood from there.

Another vivid memory happened a few years later, again in the hospital.

*"Today I woke up and got ready to go to the hospital. I had to fast again with no food or water, since I am going into the Operating room...I was disappointed to not see my normal anesthesiologist, but rather another one, as he had a major surgery to do. When I finally got to the OR, I had tears in my eyes like always. The anesthesia guy dug around in my left hand, never finding the vein. (Not even touching one!) He then tried in my right hand, digging. I was screaming, crying, and shaking. My poor doc was trying to comfort me, patting me on my tummy and trying to get me to talk to him. I tried— and I also tried to sing. I whispered a prayer through my tears to the Lord. I was quoting the verse that says that He won't allow us to be tested beyond what we can bear* (I Corinthians 10:13). *Finally, the anesthesia guy put on me that horrible, dreaded-smelling oxygen* (smells like rubber) *mask, and it had that sleepy stuff in it. I was coughing and saying how I hated that smell, but he just told me to breathe...."*(Diary #5,Sept 21, 1999).

They got the IV in once my body had gone limp with sleeping. Praise the Lord!

--------

I had to visit the hospital a lot and rather considered it to be like a prison.

*"I wanna go home. Here, student doctors come in hoping to see something wrong with me"*(Diary#1, May28, 1997).

*They would ask me, "So, are you feeling nauseous?" "No." "Have you been vomiting?" "No."(Obviously, if I'm not nauseated, why would I be vomiting! Ha-ha) "Have you been excrementing well?" and many other similar questions. "It seems that everyone enjoys it here but me. Mom, dad, Tutu—they come and read or watch TV and visit or relax"* (Diary#1, May 28, 1997).

I got to be quite known in the hospital. If I hadn't "visited" for a while, the nurses would be sad. They were always trying their best to make me feel comfortable. They had sweet smiles and cheerful words to share about their young children or some other area of their lives. They dreaded having to cause me pain, when having to start an IV or give me an injection. One time, I was in terrible pain from lying in bed so long that my nurse gave me a massage to help alleviate it. When I was too weak to get up, they'd bathe my body. When I was strong enough to have a shower, they'd help me undress (It was rather difficult with an additional "limb"—my pole.) and get the water to the right temperature. Their petite statures made it somewhat difficult to assist me, as they were often little over half my height, but they did the best they could. They'd come in the middle of the night to give me my every 6-hour injection into the IV or some anti-nausea medication. They were good to me. I had some nurses that became "experts" at finding usable veins on me, as they got to be few and far between. Mostly, it was my nurse Rosy. She was almost always there when I was. I got to know her after having her for so long. After a traumatic time in the OR, *"I was waiting a while to be taken to my room, when I heard Rosy's voice and I said, "Rosy?" Another nurse was surprised that I had recognized it. Rosy responded that we had known each other for two and a half years or so"* (Diary#5, Sept.21,1999).

One time, however, I could have been "knocked silly" by a simple accident. It was night and mom and I were sleeping when a nurse came in to replace this big, empty bottle of chemo for a glass one that was full. As she did it, the bottle fell from its holder and fell towards my face! It hit the left side of my bed, close to my head and rolled, falling onto the floor. If it had hit me, I could have been knocked unconscious and likely badly burned by the toxic chemicals, and if it had broken that would have cost a lot of money. Praise the Lord it didn't!!

> *"I went to the hospital (prison). I had quite a few unpleasant and pleasant times. The nurse found a vein (after a bit of digging with a huge size "20" needle) but the vein, which they said, was healthy and thick, exploded. Doc finally said just to take me to the operating room and they'd put it in there. I told the doc. I didn't really know for sure that doctors knew how to put in IV's. Well, the anesthesiologist put it in well and with my little (by now size "24") needle...The food was really disgusting this time. I wasn't fed much good stuff. I lost like 5 pounds!*
>
> *"I had some bad experiences with air in the tube of my IV. One was at midnight when a nurse came to give me my injection. I noticed that she was preparing the other bottle and I told her that she could put it directly into the IV (everyone else did). She said it was the same and did it her way anyway. A few minutes later, I woke up mom because my arm hurt and I had to go to the bathroom. I wanted to make sure everything was running well. There was air in the tube and it was just about going into the vein! (Maybe it already was! That is very dangerous.) Mom got the nurse. She worked at it and finally about 20-30 minutes later got everything together. I was a little scared it would get plugged. It also hurt sometimes with what she was doing. That happened on my last night. I couldn't sleep for a while* (Diary #4, March 21-23, 1999).

--------

During my treatments, my skin was extra sensitive. The chemo would cause my skin to burn more easily. Sometimes, a combination of the chemo and sun would cause my skin to break out into horrible rashes. The last few months, I had a rash on my face that itched and looked like acne that wouldn't go away. Once I was off all of this, my skin went back to normal.

The first few times I had the yellow chemo, a kind that affects the skin and digestive tract mostly, it caused my nails to break and peel. Normally, my nails were strong and long, but the chemo affected them, and so I would have to trim them to painfully short.

The worst thing about leukemia was all the treatments I had to take. We believe in divine healing and that God still heals today. We knew that God had healed me, but we never felt that we should stop the treatments. Leukemia is not like other types of cancer either, where one can see a tumor miraculously disappear. God can use doctors to heal people, too. So, I went through over 2 and a half years of treatment. It was a huge mountain to cross, but the Lord helped me. I had people all over the world praying for me. And now, as I look back, it's hard to believe I went through all of this; that this storm has passed. The Lord is good.

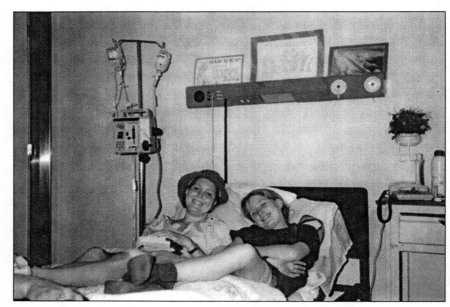

**enjoying a good visit with Ana Joy
(in hospital bed)**

# Chapter 6

# "We're All in This Together."

"Folks, we are in England and we have been requesting prayer for Arlene in every meeting. Your God and our God too is on His throne. You have been heavily on our minds today....opened the computer tonight to email you and there was your message of urgency. Be assured of our constant concern and prayers. Keep in touch, please. His mercies are new every morning. Love and prayers....Uncle and Auntie"

Beloved Arlene,

Hi, how are you? I know that you don't know me, but I'm from a youth group in Malaga, Spain. I'm writing this letter to tell you to never lose your trust in the Lord, because we all know that He is always with us. We heard about your illness and wanted you to know that we, both in our church and individual homes, are praying for you. We trust with all of our love, hope, and hearts that you'll get better soon and come out of this healed and well. I love you!"

--------

## Friends are a blessing!

*The youth from my church here and my friends and family from our church in Canada wrote me cards and prayers several times that really touched my heart. I'd like to share a few of them (many of them are translated)...*

*"Lord, I ask you to help our sister. Thank you that we are going to have the victory, because greater is He who is in me than he who is in the world!"*

*"Lord, I ask You for Arlene's life that You'll light up her path— that her hospital tests won't hurt her because we claim Arlene's life. We believe and trust that You will heal her...it's the only thing I ask."*

*"Lord, I thank you for Arlene. Help her and give her the strength to endure these tests. May she know that You'll never leave her, that You're always at her side, and know that we are here for her too."*

*"Despite everything, we were so glad to hear of your unwavering spirits in the midst of the storms of life. Praise God! <u>Arlene, you are a warrior</u>!! To hear of your songs together with your mom as you go through your painful treatments encouraged my/our hearts, I tell you! We know God is working out everything that you are going through for good as He said in His words.... Remember that God is that fourth person in your fire and He will not cause the flames to burn you, nor the waters to overflow you...."*

*"Arlene, I hope that you are doing well! We miss you!"*

*"Lord, we ask You for Arlene, that You'll give her strength to go through with these tests. We thank You for her life, because we know that everything that happens has a purpose and we know that her purpose is great. We ask that everything will*

*turn out well and that the miracle in her life will serve to save many people."*

*"Arlene, precious, precious girl—we love you so much!"*

*" Arlene, I will be praying and believing for your healing. May you be at peace in this time of blessed healing."*

*"Arlene, I will pray for you all the time."*

*" God is so good. I know without a doubt that God is going to heal you. You and Your family are such a blessing to others."*

--------

*Throughout my treatments, the people closest to me were my family. Often we only consider the person going through the pain and forget that those around them feel it too. They see you at your best and worst moments, yet still love you. Mom, dad, Michael, Tutu, and Bapa (my grandparents) witnessed my hair loss, nauseas, headaches, feebleness, crankiness at times, injections, complaints, and likely knew more the "background pressures" than I did, yet encouraged me to smile and look to Jesus. They spent countless hours taking care of me, and best of all, pouring their love into me. My mom taught me to let my tears fall, "as often they make you feel better". Because of all of this, I have asked them to put their "two-cents worth" into this book. We are very close, and found that this whole experience made us grow even closer together.*

*My mom is the first to share her thoughts and feelings as she was the one that witnessed most all of everything. She was and is still a great support to me. She and I became like best friends. Not only did she help care for me physically in the hospital, but she watched movies with me, read to me, helped me study for tests, taught me a little French, massaged me, took me to the bathroom, suffered seeing me in pain, gave me advice, and was always ready to give me a much needed hug and shoulder to cry on. She made me laugh with her silly antics and dramatizing ways, and was my most faithful visitor. I love you, mom!!*

## SING, ARLENE, SING
### Written by Rowene Sheppard

"Sing, Arlene, Sing"—this is what Arlene's doctor would plead as he proceeded to do a particularly excruciating treatment. From the very beginning of her illness, during every blood test, needle-prick of any kind or painful procedure, she was known throughout the hospital for singing praises to God as she endeavored to cope. I know because I was with her during every one of these torturous experiences.

--------

"She's beauuuutiful" was the constant reaction as friends and family saw baby Arlene for the first time. As the years went by it was obvious that she was also a very beautiful person on the inside as well. From her earliest years she loved Jesus and wanted to please Him. Many times as I would pray with her at bedtime she would ask "Mom, I said or did -----------to someone today. Was I wrong?" She always wanted to make sure that everything was right between her and God before she went to sleep at night.

When she was about 12 years old we were ministering in a church as a family in Canada. As usual, Michael and Arlene were up on the platform helping us lead worship. After the singing was over, the pastor came to the platform and remarked on the rare sense of purity that shone from Arlene. This was the type of comment we received over and over throughout the years, as lives were touched by her excellent, sweet spirit and joyful enthusiasm. As she matured, however, I became aware of a very agonizing thought: "Satan, the enemy of our souls hates her because she is everything that he hates." Although I never verbalized it, and tried to avoid thinking about it, there was an awareness that the adversary would come against her and maybe even try to kill her.

A year after our trip to Canada, we were ministering in a city four hours from home. It was Easter Sunday evening and we were on our way to the pastor's home after having celebrated two wonderful services commemorating the Lord's triumphal resurrection. Suddenly, right before our eyes we saw a huge water truck turn into our lane, giving us no warning. Within seconds we crashed, my husband, David's air bag opened, and we found the left part of the front of our Chrysler van partially under the side of the truck. Everything—eyeglasses, instruments and books went flying. Although all of the occupants of the car were shaken up and bruised, only David and Arlene sustained serious injuries. David broke his right arm and Arlene her collarbone. This accident began a year of unusual trials as we tried to continue our ministry, much of the time without a vehicle. My keyboard also had broken down and so, our usual weekend itinerant activities were greatly diminished, and at times, curtailed.

Eight months later, Arlene began to develop strange and varying symptoms. At times she would complain of pain in her ribs. Sometimes her back would ache for days. After consulting various doctors, a blood test revealed that she had a serious blood disease and the Lord directed us to Dr. Moreno. I will never forget his saying that he suspected Leukemia, but to be sure, he had to do a bone marrow test. So, up on the table she climbed, and within minutes, experienced the most piercing agony she had ever felt in her life. David and I felt our hearts torn in two, as her screams reverberated throughout the entire clinic. From the beginning, we told the doctor that we believed God would heal Arlene. He responded that of course prayer would be fine, but it would really be the "medicine" that would cure her.

As the diagnosis was confirmed, friends immediately supported us in our churches here, as well as across the world by internet. Most of the time, their reactions were encouraging and helpful. Sometimes we had to cut off their well-meaning comments mid-sentence. One of our closest friends tried to console us by saying, "She is too good for this earth. God must want her up in heaven with Him." Another acquaintance, who had recently lost her son in an accident, tried to say that we must "prepare ourselves for the worst". Needless to say, in both cases we had to break in to their exhortation with: "Thank you, but we are believing God for Arlene's complete healing."

One scripture passage that helped me greatly at that time was Luke 22: 31-32: *"And the Lord said, Simon, Simon, behold, Satan hath desired to have you, that he may sift you as wheat: But I have prayed for you that thy faith not fail and that when you have returned to me, strengthen your brethren."* I knew that when the enemy had given us his worse shot, God would somehow turn it around for our own good and be able to use us in a greater way to help others.

Our family firmly believes that when Jesus died on the cross, He bore all our sicknesses, pain and anxieties as well as our sin, and that by His stripes we were healed and made whole when we accepted Him as our Savior. The word "salvation" in the Bible also means deliverance and health, so in our hearts and minds Arlene was already healed. This truth, however, presented a great dilemma to me. Within one month of treatment, she was in complete remission, meaning that the leukemia was under control. Her blood levels were fine and she was going about life pretty much as normal. "How could we tell if there were clones of irregular white cells in her bone marrow?" Many people with gifts of healing had prayed for Arlene. In a blood cancer, however, there are no outside signs or tumors that immediately disappear, proving that healing has taken place. "Must we subject Arlene to the years of traumatic chemotherapy, with all of its terrible side affects if it may be unnecessary?" we repeatedly asked ourselves. It was because of this great uncertainty and lack of peace, that we decided to continue with the full protocol of treatment. At that point, we had no idea that it would go on for more than 4 years!

Just as Arlene was beginning to feel quite well, (although she looked a bit like a chipmunk from taking high doses of steroids for a month), we discovered that she was to enter into the most traumatic phase of treatment. During that time, her blood was brought to dangerously low levels in order to wipe out any remaining cancer cells. She spent much of her time in the hospital receiving chemotherapy or platelets. In Mexico, the nurses basically only do treatments and very little "moment by moment" daily care. Because of this, it was necessary for someone to stay with her 24 hours a day.

With only the occasional break for a few hours, I camped out in her room, filling photo albums, writing in my journal and reading, both to Arlene and myself. Sometimes I had to be her hands as she did her homework and wrote exams for school.

Arlene's resilience and courage always amazed me. Whenever she entered the hospital for chemo, she would bounce cheerily up to the nursing station and announce that she was there again and ready to go. Often, however, after a few days of debilitating chemo-therapy, she would have to be wheeled out to the car in a wheelchair, limp and weak, unable to keep her head up or walk without assis-tance. On a couple of such occasions, we were surprised when early the next morning she got up and went to school. In fact, we are very thankful that she rarely missed school due to illness. One afternoon, after a grueling session of chemo, both in her spinal fluid and by IV, she went directly to a spring concert rehearsal at her school where she stood for hours, practicing many choir songs for the program the following evening.

Probably one of the most traumatic episodes occurred when, on Mexican Mother's day, a Saturday evening, Arlene's hair almost totally fell out after she washed it. She was left practically bald with only a thin fringe of hair around the bottom. Sunday morning we frantically went around town looking for a wig which Arlene liked, but were unsuccessful. We therefore had to go to church with Arlene decked out in a hat, definitely not looking like herself. I remember crying throughout the entire service, overwhelmed by my emotions and the trauma of the evening before.

It is always heart-rending for parents to experience the suffering of their children. I now have a greater compassion and empathy for those who have loved ones going through life-threatening illness and pain. As a mother, the most difficult times for me were when Arlene was down and discouraged. On those occasions, I felt totally devastated and helpless as I tried to encourage her. Fortunately, Arlene is a very up-beat type of person so those occasions were few and far between, but I understand now the devastating pain suffered by parents of children who are unable to cope with their illness and its side affects.

For over a year after she finished her chemotherapy treatments, every time I passed the pharmacy at "Sam's Club", I felt a certain emotional heaviness in the pit of my stomach, as I remembered the monthly trips to buy her oral chemotherapy pills, and I'm thankful that it's no longer necessary. As a mom, there are moments still, when I have to fight off fearful thoughts whenever Arlene feels weak and tired or has minor illness. Thoughts that there could be a relapse try to invade my mind, and I have to remind myself of the promises of God's Word to us.

---------

More than five years have now passed since Arlene was diagnosed with Leukemia. Her doctor has pronounced her "cured", and has given her a clean bill of health. Everywhere we go she is asked: "Is that really you? We've been praying for you for years." Her young life has already inspired and encouraged many people and she is often given the opportunity to share her testimony in many different situations. Soon she plans to enter Christ for the Nations Institute in Dallas Texas, where she will go to be trained to be able to make an even greater impact on many lives.

--------------------

*My dad is the best dad in the universe! When I was little, he would take me out weekly for an ice-cream cone as a sort of "date". He is a very busy man, but has always taken the time to be with me when I needed him the most. He not only gave me life, but also gave of his life—blood—to strengthen me. His God-given administrative abilities enabled him to take care of the financial ends of my treatments, so that the rest of us didn't have to worry about it so much. Often a sweet kiss on my cheek, or gentle pat on my shoulder from my dad was just what my soul yearned for. My dad taught me, both by words and actions, that I have a Heavenly Father who loved me so much that He gave up His only Son to die on the cross for me so that I could have true life! Both of my Fathers love me so much! I am so grateful!*

Dear dad,     August 28, 2002

From the moment that I first looked into your eyes, I knew that I was looking to someone who loved and cared for me — always. I came into your life, but you came into mine and filled it with joy and love. Just as you helped me take my first steps in life, you also taught me to step out in faith for the Lord. I am forever grateful to the Lord for giving me someone to push, yet guide my "swing" through life.

I love you, dad!

Have a happy birthday!
Arlene

**DEAR DAD, AUG 28, 2002**

**PHOTO OF BABY ARLENE, HER DAD AND BROTHER**

**ANOTHER OF HER BEFORE THE MIRROR**

## ARE THERE NO DOCTORS IN THE HOSPITAL TODAY?
### Written by Arlenes's dad, David Sheppard

It may seem that dad was far away throughout all of this, but I wasn't. Being a nurse and her mother, Rowene did spend a lot of time in the hospital with Arlene. Though it had been many years since she had completed her training and work as an RN, those studies and experiences all of a sudden were paying great dividends. She really became Arlene's private nurse; literally, as at times, she was the only one there. One time, when Arlene's nose started bleeding and she couldn't stop it, she searched the entire hospital only to discover that there were no doctors available for 45 minutes or more! Being a wife, she called home to ask me what to do. I prayed quick and called up the hospital, hoping that a male voice might scare up a doctor.

*"Are there no doctors in the hospital today? How long does he need to shower? Is there no doctor even in Emergency? Her nose has been bleeding for 45 minutes! Send one up to room 401, please!"*

My work didn't end there. Countless trips and phone calls were made in order to bring some sort of stability to our lives. During one period of about 6 or 7 weeks, we were privileged to have Rowene's mom, also an RN of many years, come and live somewhere between the hospital and our home. She helped out in so many ways, even allowing Rowene a few "hours off" to be able to get out of the hospital room. Rowene would go home, bath and get some fresh clothes to wear and maybe a decent meal. There was a time I was every two or three days getting extensions on mother-in-law's airline ticket to allow her to stay a few more days to help with Arlene.

On more than one occasion, I can remember baring my arm to give blood, too. Our son was only 16, but he and I both went that first time when there was an emergency. More than once we asked members of our Mexican church for blood donors. One Sunday morning, I can remember asking for 20 blood donors and some 22 "Mexican friends" quickly stood to their feet to volunteer. Another time, when she suffered so and needed pints of blood or else a donor with the same blood type that would give a quantity of just platelets, I got the call. They were looking to me for help.

*"What am I to do? Where am I to go?"*

*" Go to the hospital across town, see Doctor such an such, and he'll put you on the plasmaphoresis machine where they'll spin the platelets out of your blood and then run your blood back into the other arm,"* was the command.

*Oh, OK, I'll do it.* It was quite the ordeal. My blood looked rather anemic as they pumped it back into my body. They took 17or 19 units of platelets that day from me, but that was 17 or 19 liters of blood Arlene's body didn't have to deal with. I did it once for my daughter and then twice more at later dates trying to help a young man that Arlene had met who also was dying with an even more aggressive type of leukemia. What is life if you can't at least try to help another more needy than your self?

Then there were the moments of anxious prayers, the phone calls and e-mails, the trips to the hospital 2 or 3 times a day, the corner store, the bank, the explanations as to why another $2500 or $4500 US when I just got a large quantity a few days before. There was the believing for, and at times the arranging for and receiving of all that money, getting it exchanged into pesos, filling out hospital admission forms and insurance forms, paying the hospital, the doctors, the blood bank, etc. I was busy too! But one thing we can testify, when one puts his or her whole trust in the Lord God, He will not fail you. Look what He has done for us. He can do it again for you too. Trust Him one day at a time. There is hope when we trust in God.

--------------

*This section was written after Arlene passed away so it does not include a personal introduction from her. It is written by Michael, Arlene's brother.*

The thing about our feelings is that sometimes we can't describe them and yet at other times when we just don't want it to; it hurts too much. For example, the feelings that I lived through as I sat at home one night just watching the television. My sister hadn't felt very well so my parents had taken her to get a check up. Everything was calm, even peaceful as I heard my dad drive into the carport. But that silence was broken, not by the sound of the show I was watching but by an ear piercing scream as she got out of the van. I could not believe that that sound could come from my sister. She was still outside and you'd think that I, a curious brother, would get up and see what had happened. But it seemed that all I could do was just sit there, stupefied as my mom carefully led my sister past me and into her bedroom. My sister was hunched over and reminded me of one of those old ladies that a gentleman would lead across the street. But this was no old woman walking into our home, it was my sister. A new chapter was being written into the book of our lives.

It is no secret that this changed our lives for good. Arlene went through the pain and the humiliation of losing her hair many times. She endured treatment after treatment. Her body changed and sometimes it was hard to look at her and call her "Gorgeous," which I often did anyway. But I knew, as well as everyone that knew her, that underneath all of the pain, the bloating of her skin and lack of hair, there was a girl; a woman of God and one of the best of people.

Time went on and it was soon summer. Ah, the time to relax and enjoy the good weather and most importantly, freedom from school. It happened that that summer I went up to Christ for the Nations, a Bible college in Dallas, Texas. I had the privilege of working at their summer youth camp. I also went there to see a girlfriend who lived there. Although I tried to keep in contact with my family while I was there I was also trying to escape from the pain and suffering that she was going through by being away. But during this time Arlene became quite ill. She had a really bad fever for about a week and she also had a really bad nose bleed that didn't want to heal. She was weak and maybe even dying! Thoughts plagued my mind and questions arose. Questions of God, of life, and of purpose. "How can this be happening to her and not to me? I'm the bad one, not her!" "What am I doing here?" "Why am I even here?" "Should I leave?" "But I don't have the money to change my ticket." "Lord, what should I do?" And there I was, just stuck there while my one and only sister might die.

It is in those times of storm we have but few options. We can just give up, letting the waves sweep us overboard into the raging sea where we sink to the depths of despair and finally death. But how could I do this when my sister herself wouldn't let any circumstance get her down. We can just try and hold the ship together, but that ultimately fails because the wind is too strong, the waves too deep, and the ship is too big for you to control. The only way of salvation is to call on a savior; someone to rescue us from what we cannot handle. For He is not only the master and commander, but also the Creator. Jesus is the only one who can say to waves, "Be still!" And to the winds, "Be silent!" But how can He do that if we won't make Him our captain , our master and Lord? He can't. Therefore we must cling to the only one who is firm, trustworthy and true.

--------------

*My grandma is one of my favorite people in the world! She and I also grew especially close through these ordeals as she was with me a lot, too. Ah, we shared a lot of good laughs despite pain and discomfort. When I was in "house arrest", not being able to leave the house, she'd stay home with me from church and we'd have our own time of prayer and devotion. Then we'd often play a rousing game of UNO or Dutch Blitz. She'd gently hold me when I'd pour out my heart in tears, make me laugh other times, and even give me injections at home\*, so that I didn't have to be taken into the clinic. My grandma is a very dignified-type lady, but also knows how to laugh and cheer up the world.*

*My grandpa is someone whom I deeply admire. He also is good at spreading laughter with his witty jokes and playful ways. He is a real man of God, too, and I know that he spent many hours praying for me. He's the type of person that can spend all day in our back-yard, meditating on the Word of God. If you go out there with him, you'll usually end up receiving some "nuggets" and interesting insights from the Bible. My grandpa is also very gentle. I remember the time that they came to the hospital to visit me for the first time... He lovingly put his hand under my chin and held back his tears as mine broke through.*

(\* Arlene's grandmother is a retired registered nurse with many years of experience.)

--------

## Written by Ken and Ruth Stevenson

As I write this, I am thinking back over four years. We, Arlene's Grandma and Grandpa (Tutu and Bapa), were planning a trip down to Puebla, Mexico, to visit our daughter, Rowene, her husband, David, and their two children, Michael, 16, and Arlene, 14. We were scheduled to fly down on April 1, 1997. Arlene had not been well for several months, but a day or two before we were to leave, Rowene phoned to say that Arlene had been diagnosed with leukemia. Of course, we were devastated but could see it was God's plan for us to be able to be with our loved ones and give them whatever support we could. When we arrived in Puebla about 10 p.m., we went directly to the hospital to see Arlene, who had been started on chemotherapy. It was necessary for Rowene to stay at the hospital with Arlene, as that is the custom in Mexico.

I should say that our immediate reaction when hearing of Arlene's diagnosis was that she should be brought home to Canada for the best treatment. I have since seen that that wasn't God's plan. God provided one of the best Pediatric Oncologists, Dr. Moreno, in the country for her. She also had the love and support of all her friends in the Puebla church, who prayed for her and gave their blood for her when needed. After three weeks or so, we returned to Canada as planned, but I felt strongly that I was to return to Mexico. So after a few days at home to attend to some necessary business, I went back to Puebla. These were very difficult days for all of us. I tried to help wherever I could, either at home washing clothes, getting meals etc., or spelling Rowene off at the hospital so she could go home for awhile. There were times that things were very critical and all we could do was call on God for mercy. Rowene and I spent many hours sponging Arlene's body with cold cloths trying to bring her high temperature down. With the long period of high fever, her muscles just wasted away and she was unable to walk. I was scheduled to return to Canada, but I knew I couldn't leave so had my flight changed a number of times until I felt free to go. It was a difficult time at home in Canada for "Bapa" who could only pray for Arlene and hope also that I would be able to return soon. One of the happiest times for him was when he was able to talk to Arlene, herself on the telephone and know that she was improving.

During these difficult weeks there were many times when I questioned God, "How could this happen to a girl who loved You so much and to a family who had given everything in order to serve You"? or " Why should this happen to our Granddaughter? We have served You these many years."

I came to realize that God had allowed this illness for a reason. He would bring good out of it. I saw the Mexican young people in the church, bonded together in prayer for Arlene. I saw people who traveled long distances on buses in order to pray for her. I saw God miraculously provide finances to cover all the heavy expenses of Arlene's treatment. I sometimes wondered why we didn't have the necessary faith to see Arlene healed immediately and be spared the painful protocol she had to endure.

Then I read of the many heroes of faith in Hebrews chapter 11. Some of these heroes didn't "escape" but had faith to endure torture, jeering, flogging, chains, stoning, death by the sword, persecution, etc. These were all commended for their faith. We would all like to escape hardship or sickness, but it also takes faith to endure these things.

We praise God for bringing Arlene through this trial and praise Him that she is being used to minister healing compassion to others going through situations similar to hers and that her testimony will be influential in bringing many people into the Kingdom. We (Tutu and Bapa) will always remember arriving late in the evening, having been picked up at the Mexico City Airport by David and Rowene. As we arrived at their home, Arlene came running out to meet us. I (Bapa) will never forget her bald head against my cheek. The tears were flowing as she said, *"Oh, Bapa, I'm so glad you came!"*

--------------

Arlene suffered much in the following months, having lost her hair a total of 8 times.

Even without hair, she was a stunningly attractive girl. Today, by the Grace of God, she is truly beautiful and has an inner beauty that comes from her close relationship with her Lord and from a meek and quiet spirit.

--------

*I would like to share with those of you who are family members of someone with leukemia or another life-threatening disease: never give up hope! If you encourage and love the person suffering with the illness, you'll find that not only he or she will feel better, but you will too! I know that it must be difficult at times, but look to Jesus—trust me, it works!*

**Arlene and her daddy**

**Arlene & Bapa in garden chairs**

**Rowene, Tutu & Arlene**

# Chapter 7

# "Lupita"

--------

" Hey Arlene,

It is my hope that this card will encourage you and put
your mind at rest. God says in His Word that He commands
His angels to guard over us. You know, I wouldn't be
surprised that in really tough times, He will send a whole
army of angels to bring us comfort.

So, I hope that now, through this card you remember that
God cares greatly about you, and has sent angels to hold you
up in your time of weakness. And we care for you also. We,
your friends, are here to help the angels whenever we can.
Please don't hesitate to call on us at anytime. We love you
and hope that you get well soon. Remember to look toward
heaven when all else fails. May God keep you (I'm here
whenever you need anything)."

--------

When I was going through all these treatments, enduring excruciating pains, losing my hair, etc. I could have gone around
moping and feeling sorry for myself. However, one thing we find

as we live this life is that there will always be others worse off than us. I may have suffered a lot, but there are people who suffer far more. We see that many are starving, are being constantly abused, are blind, are paralyzed, are always in pain, and the list goes on and on. Sometimes we find little children who have gone through the mill before they are even old enough to know what's happening to them. Such was the case of my friend Lupita.

One time when I was taking a treatment in the clinic, my nurse, Marta, told me about this little bundle of sunshine and energy, Lupita. She had a form of stomach cancer and lived in a nearby town. I was anxious to meet this three-year old girl. Well, one day I was given the honor. She was the first person I met with cancer since I was diagnosed. *"I met Lupita! She's a cute, sweet, pretty little girl. She has very short, black hair and wore a pretty dress and a sweet smile" (Diary #1, June 9, 1997).* This little person had gone through countless amounts of radiation therapy and chemotherapy in her short life.

We often had our treatments coincide, and so I would get to visit her in the hospital. We, alongside our IV posts, would sit there to chat.

*"Arlene, I have this cow named Canada. And uh, another one named Esperanza* (Hope)." she would tell me about them and awarded me often with her smile. One time, I brought her a bunch of children's books and little toys for her to enjoy. I remember her lying on her bed as we played together with a pop-up book. We had our little people, Barbie and company, and we would take them to the school, and put them to bed, feed them and do all of the necessary "house" play. She really had fun and I did, too, seeing her and playing with her. Her company was a great blessing to me; it would help me forget about myself and my pain and focus on her. Another time, I was awaiting the call to go into the doctor's office to get my bone marrow test and back shot. Jitters filled my stomach. I tried to distract myself by studying for a Biology exam but to no avail. Then along came Lupita. We began to talk and I showed her animal pictures from my Biology book. Once again, she helped me not to think about the inevitable injections.

She was so little, only three years old. Dark eyes and a mouth full of baby teeth and lips full of joyful smiles adorned her face. Most of the time she was bald. Lupita was beautiful and I loved her bald head. It was normal for me to see her bald. She was so precious to me and I loved her dearly.

I remember one time when she complimented me on my earrings. She, along with so many other children, enjoyed watching the fish swim in my animated watch. It makes me cry as I remember this.

Every time that my mom and I visited Lupita in the hospital, we asked to pray for her. On many occasions, her family, forgetting about her doctor's appointments, would bring her to my doctor half-dead. He would then have to do his best to give her life again. However, one time in particular the situation was hopeless. The doctors no longer knew what to do. She was in Intensive Care. We received a phone call from her mom. *"Rowene, can you please come and pray for our little Lupita. She is in Intensive care..."* They weren't religious people, but nonetheless they invited us. My mom and I went right away. God specializes in the impossible. Only one person at a time was allowed in to visit her. When my turn came, I got all gowned and masked up, but these physical preparations did nothing to prepare me for what I would see. I walked into the little room, where this single bed held my precious friend. The bed looked enormous because of her tiny form. Massive machines and tubes were connected to her all around. She was sedated as her head had begun to bleed internally, but when I walked in, her eyes fluttered open, recognizing my presence in the room. I said, *"Hola, Lupita. I love you so much and so does God."* I prayed for her, shed some tears, and left. The very next day, we received a phone call from my nurse, *"It's a miracle!! Lupita is out of Intensive Care and in a normal room recuperating!"* Exuberant, my mother and I went to visit her in the hospital. She had open sores all over her body from the advance of the disease and heavy radiation and chemotherapy treatment. She had to have a colostomy, too. The first solid food she ate was one of my mom's homemade oatmeal cookies. We were so thankful for the life that God restored to her and we were blessed with her presence for a while longer. A few months later she died.

However, I did not find out about her death until six months later. My doctor didn't even know about it. I asked hospital personnel about her and most didn't know anything about how she was doing. One man told me she had died, but we could not believe him. How could she die without her doctor's knowledge? Eventually, my mom got Lupita's phone number and called. The man had been right. She had died. The family must have given up hope, and decided not to put her through any more suffering.

Her death caused me much grief. I would cry every so often for months. It affected me more than my own Grandma Sheppard's death. How could someone so young, just barely starting her life, die? My grandma had lived a full life, but Lupita didn't get the chance. Then, the Lord helped me realize that she was really in a better place. I would envision her in a puffy pink dress and ribbons, dancing around in heaven with Jesus, laughter and smiles filling the atmosphere. Then she would be wrapped in Jesus' arms, and I knew she was much better off. She was no longer in pain. No more difficult treatments. No more open sores. No more fevers. No more doctors and hospitals. She's already spending all eternity with Jesus. She is blessed as I am as well for having known her.

# Chapter 8

# "Carlos"

*"What a privilege we have been given by God
to be able to spend our lives
giving His love away." —Don Lessin*

During my treatments, I had a great desire to meet someone my age with leukemia. When I would scream and cry out in agony in a particularly painful injection or treatment, my dear, sweet mother, who suffered with me would say, " I understand, Lovey." I would shoot back at her, " No you don't understand, mom." A person can never fully comprehend a situation until they, too, go through it. That's why I so desperately needed a friend my age, who'd feel the pain of "going bald" in your teen years. And Carlos stepped into my life...

"Ok, Arlene, you practice this scale one more time; I have to go get a book. I'll be right back," said Miguel, my flute teacher.

Knock, knock! "Hey, I want you to meet someone!" exclaimed mom. "Arlene, this is Carlos. He has leukemia and is sixteen years old."

There, before my eyes, was a young guy wearing a hat similar to some that I had. His face was puffy too!

"I'm Arlene. It's nice to meet you!" Thank, You, Lord!! "
So, what you doing here at the music academy?"

"Oh, I'm studying music theory and the guitar. I love
music; I also enjoy writing it with a friend of mine," Carlos
responded.

*Wow! He's even into music like I am!! Thanks God!!*

The Lord gave me the answer to my prayer for a friend who'd
really understand what I was going through. Carlos was only two
weeks older than me, so you couldn't ask for someone "more my
age". He and his family were actually from Mazatlán, but had
moved to Puebla so that his dad could get his Master's degree at the
University of the Americas. Some missionaries had told us about
this man who studied there and had a son with leukemia, and had
wanted to introduce us. Later we found out that it was the same
person!!

Carlos had a much more severe type of leukemia; the most
aggressive kind. It is basically incurable. He had eighty percent
cancer cells in his blood. Eventually, he went blind. That didn't stop
his joy. He became paralyzed. That couldn't steal it, either. When
his speech became 'impaired' and slurred from his condition, he still
managed to tell jokes. I would visit him in the hospital, going to try
to cheer him and his family up, but would end up being encouraged
myself! The reason why he was able to maintain his exuberant spirit
is because he knew the secret: "The joy of the Lord is my strength"
(Nehemiah 8:10b). Carlos knew Jesus as his Savior; therefore, he
had an overabounding supply of joy.

*I had my flute lesson and I met this guy named Carlos who
is 16, has leukemia.... Oh, he has a lot of faith and prays for
people and they get healed!"* (Diary #4, January 28, 1999).

--------

*"Today, mom and I went to visit Carlos in the hospital.
The hospital was dark and dingy. The "guards" only let*

*one person up to see patients at a time. We thought that one person could go up and get someone down, so that we could all go up. I told mom to go up. I waited alone for about 25 minutes! Bored, I entertained myself by imagining that the horrible hospital was not a hospital but a prison camp or prison. 'The lady looks innocent, but really is an axe-murderer; the old man is the jail keeper'—that sort of stuff. It was fun. I also prayed for mom that she hadn't gotten lost. I thought about "convincing" the guard to let me through with force. Like saying, 'Hey Mister, I know what it is like being in a hospital for hours and days and it is boring! And this hospital is terrible.' But I didn't and also concluded that Jesus wouldn't push His way through and say those things. One other thing that stopped me from doing that was that I thought, 'What if they come down and can't find me?'*

"*At one point, I got up to look at this wall with pictures on it. I found they all shared the theme of women's breasts and was a bit embarrassed. I resumed my vigil. When I finally got to go up, mom had to stay down and I went by myself into this slow, mental-institution-like elevator. I went to Carlos' room—3 beds in a room. There was no TV and just enough space for the bed with a tiny space around it. Michelle (his sister) and Carlos (of course) were there. He said the test he had turned out negative—that's good. However, he still has symptoms like he can't talk well, etc. I got him to play and sing a song he wrote with a friend on his guitar. It was good, what I could understand of it. The room had no bathroom. I couldn't stay long, so I ventured down. The elevator was taking so long to come and I saw no lights, so I wondered if it was working—I even asked. I was just going to take the stairs (after asking if the dark stairs would take me to the same place), when the elevator came...Being at the place Carlos was at sure makes me thankful for my hospital where I'm spoiled. I mean that place could depress anyone even if they weren't even going to stay!*" (Diary #4, February 2, 1999)

Carlos spent a lot of time in the hospital because his case was so serious. The last 3 months of his life were spent cooped up in a tiny, simple room. His mother slept on the floor under his bed. Sometimes, his sister stayed there as well.

" *We were going to go grocery shopping when we passed by Carlos's hospital. I asked if he was still there and if we could stop by. We went in and saw Beatrice* (his mother) *with tears in her eyes waiting downstairs for their doctor. I went up and had a hard time finding Carlos' room; I guess he was in intensive care type stuff since he had his own room... I think Carlos had a fever, as he was sweating and was only wearing boxers. We took turns fanning him. Mom talked with Beatrice while I was up there. Carlos had a spiky head of hair, and could hardly stay awake; though he still laughed a bit. He even asked me if I was going to the café on Friday. I said 'yes' and he said 'see you there' type thing. We found out he has 80% blasto, cancer cells. He had an oxygen mask to help him breathe, was receiving platelets, had petechiae. He needs a miracle.* (Diary #4, April 6, 1999). A few days later, "*Today we went to visit Carlos. His blood report turned out to be great news! He had 0% blastos, 10 hemoglobin, and 40,000 platelets. Considerably good. Praise the Lord!*" (Diary #4, April 9,1999)

His mother was always running around looking for blood donors. Several times, my dad went to give of his precious supply of blood through a very expensive process, called Plasmapherisis, in order to produce concentrated amounts of platelets.

He was a real joker. He'd always tease my friend that one night he'd go to her house and devour her cats. Other times, he told so many jokes, we could hardly stop laughing. His family was so nice to me; they even gave me a card and some chocolates for Valentine's Day. (His life inspired me.) "*We found out yesterday that Carlos is bad—again. His brain might have been hemorrhaging. Poor guy. He's been in the hospital for six weeks straight, in pain, blind, brain bleeding, nose bleeding—lots of stuff, but still holding onto his faith and laughing!!! Oh!"* (Diary#4, May 13, 1999)

--------

One night...

*"I got home, and was taking off my makeup when the phone rang. Then dad told me that Beatrice and José were kicked out of the room because Carlos was dying....I started crying. I finally got into bed and sobbed. I thought everyone had gone to bed when...the phone rang. We learned that Carlos had passed on to heaven...we asked them if we could do anything to help...they just wanted us there...We got to the dark hospital and up to Beatrice and José. The first thing they said to us was that they were having a party. However, Beatrice at least did cry. I asked if I could go see Carlos. José asked me if I was feeling up to it. I got mom and dad to go with me. What I saw I had not expected.... He looked like a mummy. He was completely covered up in bed wraps. I asked if I could see his face...she lifted the wraps. It was a dead, frozen Carlos; no smiles, laughs, or jokes. They had stuffed his nose, too—talk about mummified! I covered his face again. They had to move out of the room, so they were busy packing up their home, of 2-3 months. Beatrice laid on the body a pair of new cord pants that she had bought for him and then put them away. I remember seeing her, at one point turn towards the window and start sobbing quietly.... Just hours before, we had prayed for him. Just hours before we had talked about mom and I or dad coming to take care of Carlos, so that the family could go to José's gradua-tion... They gave me a tiny, school picture of him, but he isn't smiling in it! Carlos always had a story to tell, a joke, or a laugh to share.... Well, when he was conscious. People loved him; he was a great person. He was the perfect example of how the inside is the important thing...and Carlos had the*

*love of Jesus inside. Carlos we love you!"* (Diary #5, June 4/5, 1999).

The Lord answered my prayer. He gave me a friend who could understand what I was going through. His family is precious to us. We will always have a special place for them in our hearts.

# Arlene's date with *prince charming*

When 17-year-old wish child, Arlene Sheppard, visited London from Mexico recently to meet her Prince, she declared "if I had to go home now I would be truly happy".

Arlene, who has leukaemia, 'wished' to see The Prince of Wales' and when His Royal Highness asked why she wanted to meet him her response was that, 'Since I was very small you have always been my hero.' His Royal Highness very graciously found time in his hectic schedule to meet Arlene and as the day unfolded it was clear that he had taken the utmost care over Arlene's visit.

Canadian born Arlene lives in Mexico with her missionary family, father David and mother Rowene. When she first 'wished', she was told that the likelihood of meeting The Prince of Wales was slim. However, Make-A-Wish Foundation® UK, in response to a wish assist request from its Canadian and Mexican affiliates has made her 'wish' come true and arranged for the family, joined by Arlene's 20 year old brother Michael (who is currently studying theology at a Canadian university), to have a private audience with the Prince. It was planned that the audience would be ten minutes but the conversation flowed so freely that it soon turned into half an hour.

To make Arlene's wish come true many hours of travelling were involved. Arlene, David and Rowene travelled from Mexico to meet up with Michael in Chicago for an onward flight to Heathrow. However, disaster struck at Chicago when they discovered that their flight to London had been cancelled and the alternative flight offered would make them miss their Buckingham Palace visit.

A disappointed Arlene told airport officials that she would be late for her appointment with the Prince at Buckingham Palace, but no one could

believe her. After several 'phone calls Virgin Airlines came to the rescue with a first-class flight to Heathrow for the family and a chauffeur driven car to the Copthorne Tara hotel in London.

Next day the family, accompanied by Make-A-Wish®

trustee Ernita Beasley, arrived at Buckingham Palace by taxi where they were met by palace staff who walked slowly in front of the car, across the quadrangle, to the red carpet. The VIPs were then shown to the staterooms normally reserved for visiting heads of state, reflecting that President Clinton had been in the very rooms on his last visit.

During her audience with the Prince the teenager presented him with a gold Make-A-Wish® wishbone tie-pin, a lamp from Mexico and a special music tape that the family had recorded themselves.

The family then enjoyed a private tour of the palace, with a private viewing of the gift shop and an extra special visit to the Royal Mews, where they were shown around all the carriages. The highlight of this part of the visit was that one of the horses was turned round for Arlene to pet – something that does not usually happen.

A very tired and extremely happy Arlene returned to her hotel that evening after her remarkable day at the palace.

During the rest of this VIP trip to London, the family had a private tour of the Tower of London and the Crown Jewels, conducted by the Chief Yeoman, a private tour of the Natural History Museum, VIP treatment at Madam Tussaud's, a visit to the London Aquarium, a London Bus tour and a visit to the Dome. However, before they could visit the Phantom of the Opera, Arlene just had to have a facial at Harrods.

For this Wish child, Arlene, her meeting with His Royal Highness, The Prince of Wales, was truly 'her Wish come true'. She felt like a princess for a day and although the rest of her visit was absolutely tremendous her greatest memory is of the day she met the charming Prince.

**Make A Wish magazine –
Arlene's date with Prince Charming**

**Arlene & George in front of Royal Carriage**

**Family with Christina in front of
Buckingham palace gates**

**Arlene & HRH Prince Charles**

# Chapter 9:

# "From Bed to Buckingham..."

--------

**From Make a Wish BC and Yukon:**

It was an absolute pleasure to be a part of Arlene's wish to meet Prince Charles. From the day we got the referral and talked to Arlene, we knew, if we could pull it off, this would be a wish experience of a lifetime. Arlene's excitement was contagious; after speaking with her we were all the more inspired to make this brave young woman's wish a reality. Thanks to our affiliate in the UK and the generosity of many, Arlene's wish did come true. Arlene's personal journey through the life-threatening realities of cancer treatment has left her with a courageous and joyful nature. Her story, like Arlene herself, is an expression of thanksgiving and hope in times of uncertainty. Arlene's wish was truly an example of the Make-A-Wish desire for every wish we grant, to *enrich the human experience with hope, strength, and joy.*

*Brooke McAllister, Wish Grantor*
*The Make-A-Wish Foundation of BC & YK*

--------

Make a wish, and see what happens....poof! Did it appear? How often do we sigh a wish and see it actually come to pass? Many children lie on their hospital beds not knowing what tomorrow may bring, wishing that they could live a bit longer in order to have their dreams come true. (How many dream, but don't live long enough to reach it?) Well, there does exist a group of people who's mission is just that—to make sick children's wishes come true. Make a Wish Foundation is made up of an incredible team of volunteers who work their hardest to grant a wish to a child, under eighteen, who is suffering from a terminal disease. Through many charitable organizations and help from individuals, they are striving to reach the goal of giving one wish a day. During my treatments, I was contacted by this wonderful foundation....

### In the Republic of Texas

" Hello, David, Rowene, and Arlene! Why don't you guys come on up now and share a bit about what the Lord is doing in your lives,"

said Pastor Venita from our church in McAllen, Texas. This church of around 1,000 members had been praying and fasting for me, during some of our most difficult struggles. We walked up and shared about how God was healing me and providing our every need. After church, a representative from the "Make a Wish Texas" came up to us and offered me a wish.

"Well, Arlene, we'd really like for y'all to come visit us down at the office to discuss this further. How's Monday sound?"

So, we had our appointment set and as the day grew near, I had to think of what I wanted to ask for. I felt a bit selfish asking for something for me, and thought that maybe I should ask for money or something to help other kids with. Then I was told that this is for me, that the thought was quite honorable, but that this time it was my turn to be blessed. I decided to ask big, as I know my God is all-Sovereign and I knew what I wanted....

"I want to go to London and meet royalty."

"Oh, um, we aren't able to grant trips outside of the United States because of insurance policies. Do you have an alternative wish?"

"Maybe it'd be nice to go to Disneyworld in Florida."

"That would be great, many of our children choose that. Now, we just need to fill out some forms...OK, let's see... where were you born?"

"Vancouver, Canada," I replied.

"Canada?! Oh, you're not an American citizen?"

"No."

"I'm sorry. I'm afraid we'll have to put you in contact with the Canadian sector."

A bit disappointed to have this prolonged, we later found it to be a blessing in disguise....

## "Oh, Canada..."

After a few complications, I was at last able to meet with a Canadian representative, while I was in Vancouver Children's Hospital a year later, receiving one of my treatments. A very nice lady came to visit me and gave me a nice, red hat from the Olympics and talked to me about my wish. That's when things began to be guided together noticeably by my loving Father. The hidden blessing was beginning to be opened up...

"Yes, it would be fine for you to travel overseas to London. We'll try our best with the royalty, too. Oftentimes, our kids want to meet someone important or famous."

Another year passed, before everything was almost in order for us to fly to jolly 'ole' England. However, the royalty part of the wish was not shaping up. Apparently, they never do this kind of thing. But, my God specializes in the "Nevers..."

### Never say 'never'

We had just decided to go to London and have a wonderful time anyway. Our tickets were bought and everything was ready when we received a life-changing phone call from a very excited Make a Wish representative just ten days before our set arrival.

"Arlene, you've got an audience with Prince Charles!!! The Make a Wish UK sure helped pull this together." (So, did my God.)

Later I asked mom,

"Isn't Prince Charles, the next king?!!"
"Yes, darling."
"WOW!!!!!! AHHHHHH!!! Praise the Lord! That's so awesome!! But, what am I gonna wear?!"

Mom and I went shopping for a dress, but didn't find any that were "appropriate" for the occasion. Finally, we consulted with our pastor's wife about it. She said that she and her daughter could make me one. So, I chose a dress, picked out the cloth, was measured, and they had the dress ready for me in a week's time! It was perfect for the very important date; it was beautiful.

### Lost in Chicago?

Mom, dad, and I were to fly from Mexico City to Chicago, where my brother, Michael, was to meet up with us from Vancouver. We got there safely and were thrilled to be able to hug and kiss my brother. We left to go check in our luggage when we found out.

"You're flight to London, via British Airways has been canceled, and you will be informed of any other changes."

Thanking God for the Victory, we said,

> "Oh, but we come with the Make a Wish Foundation (and the most-powerful God) and must get to London, because we have an audience with Prince Charles tomorrow!"

God really spoiled us now...after verifying that we were with the Foundation, they booked us with Virgin Atlantic Airlines, one of the ritziest airlines, AND promoted us to first or Upper class!!

Aboard the plane, after having a 'revival' snack for the upper class, we enjoyed settling into the big, lazy-boy-type, leather seats. We each received a 'gift' that was made up of a couple of pouches full of toiletries, mints, socks, a pen and a notebook, a little lock, etc. Right away, we were mesmerized by the English accents surrounding us, already enjoying ourselves fully. Before we had even started flying, a pretty blond lady came to ask us if we would like to have a massage during the flight. We eagerly signed up for one. They explained to us that during the flight, we could eat however much, whenever we wanted, of whatever we chose. We were getting the royal treatment and loved every second of it. The flight itself was a mini-vacation. Ha-ha. My brother and I noticed that we all had our own TV and were intent on figuring out what we wanted to watch. After supper, we were quite full, so waited until later to have our dessert. At three a.m., he and I ordered a Belgium waffle covered with chocolate and vanilla ice cream with chocolate sauce drizzled all over. It was so good, that my parents decided to order one too.

Having landed in Heathrow airport, we had another 'revival' service, where we could order whatever we wanted for breakfast and could even shower if we wanted to. Then, a nice Volvo (limousine service) took us to our hotel, as, because of the flight changes, we had gotten to London earlier than expected, so Make a Wish wasn't able to welcome us there.

Driving through town, I immediately fell in love with London and its' architecture. It all seemed like a fairy tale. We had to adjust ourselves to driving on the "wrong side" of the road, too. Upon arrival at our hotel, exhausted, we each decided to rest awhile in our respective rooms. (I had my own room!!! I've never had my own room before at a hotel!) Later, at the Mozart café, in our hotel, we met Kelly and Ernita from Make a Wish UK for tea. Vivaciously they informed us of our itinerary, and clued us in on all of the details, including the protocol for being around Prince Charles.

"Prince Charles doesn't like to be treated differently, around young people especially. Talk to him normally. Relax. The only thing you can't do is to shake his hand or touch him in any way unless he initiates. Also, don't sit down until he has sat down, " said Ernita. " We'll meet you with a cab at 10:00 o'clock sharp."

## The Big Day

That morning, we had a nice breakfast with Ernita and later rushed in order to get all "dolled" up for our exciting day. Once in the cab, we delightedly told the driver to take us inside Buckingham Palace. Astonished, he quickly set off. As the gates of the Palace were opened for our cab, people all over were staring at us, wondering who we were. A Palace assistant, walked in front of our cab, guiding us to the right entrance. When I stepped out of the cab, I stood erect like a princess, and all the people who were waiting to tour the place, wondered what princess I was. Ha-ha. It was so much fun. We were escorted through some of the palace to the dignitaries' room, where we were to meet the prince. For about 45 minutes, we were allowed to roam the adjoining rooms freely and drink tea out of teacups inscribed with "ERII" ("Elizabeth Regina II") on them and eat little royal biscuits. The bedroom and bathroom, where we walked, and which we used and enjoyed were where people like President Clinton stay! Paintings and other antiques adorned the rooms, gifts from all over the world, and large windows, displaying the huge back gardens, which would probably warmly filter the sun through on a hot day. Michael and I admired an old desk, one which had probably served many dignitaries through the decades, signing life-changing documents. A small table held around 10 books about the palace, a gift from Prince Charles, for us. Anxiously, we awaited the Prince, until he graced the room with his presence at last! Right away, he walked up to me, shook my hand and proceeded to shake Ernita, Mom, Dad, and Michael's hands. He then sat down in a chair in front of us and we, likewise, sat down on the couches.

"I can't believe that you actually wanted to meet me!" exclaimed Prince Charles.

He was really easy to talk to—amiable and down-to earth, too. He had the grace to ease any nerves away and we conversed freely about my trip and the different places I'd be visiting. Ernita, who came with us said,

"Your highness, Arlene would like to tell you a little about her treatments and how her faith has helped her get through them."

By the time I had finished sharing, we all had tears in our eyes, including the Prince. The Presence of God was there in a very special way pouring down His anointing on me. It was breathtaking.

Our audience with Prince Charles was to last only for ten minutes, however our conversation was flowing so freely, that it lasted half an hour. Before he left, we gave him some gifts—an exquisite, flicker lamp made out of the traditional pottery, "Talavera", from Puebla, a music CD that our family had recorded, and a gold Make a Wish tie-pin. The Prince graciously received these saying, " I'm the one that should be giving you a gift!!" He was so touched, that he took me by the shoulders and planted a kiss on both of my cheeks. Quickly, we were allowed to take a picture with him—the only one permitted inside of the Palace. Then my dream day continued with a private tour of the Palace. The guard rails were taken away, so that we could walk down the royal red carpet, while the tourists continued to watch us in awe...We got in on a lot of the palace "secrets" –secret doors etc., and felt very blessed.

"Look mom, everything is blue!" I comment.

"Oh, well, yes, that is why this room is called the blue room," said Christine, the special access supervisor to the Palace, our guide.

"Ah, yes, and this is the music room, where private concerts are performed for the Queen. As you can see, that balcony overlooks the garden," continued Christine.

We were totally star-eyed by the beauty of the place. My brother, however, found the palace a little too full of naked statues. Ha-ha.

We were allowed to shop for souvenirs in the exclusive, inside shop. Everything was gorgeous and we ended up spending a lot of money in that shop. We were told, that after being in there, all of the other London store souvenirs would appear junky. I spent all of the hundred pounds given to me by the foundation for spending in that one shop. We bought a lot of special china and other trinkets like Buckingham Palace tea bags and biscuits, pens and other such like. It was a delight. We walked out of the Palace feeling like royalty.

From there, we took a lot of pictures of the front side and my brother and I "reported" the news of our experiences to our video camera. We also watched the palace guards do their rounds. Apparently, during these few days, the Royal Canadian Mounted Police Force of Canada were the guards. How interesting....

Then we were taken to the Royal Mews, where Ernita and Kelly, who had caught up with us, asked them if we could be given a tour, explaining our situation. George, our tour guide of the Mews, was a jolly sort, dressed in a black top hat and a long red coat. At first, he didn't believe that we had truly been with Prince Charles, but once he did, he let everyone know it!

"Yes, our VIP of the day."

"This young lady, here, was just with the Prince."

We even found a cement tile in the ground there with "A. Shepard" on it—quite close to my name, to make it extremely interesting....

Yes, I truly did have a dream day, but the fun didn't end there. Wherever we visited, we jumped "cues" and had private tours. From

Madame Tussaud's Wax Museum, National History Museum, Tower of London, Millennium Dome, to facials at Harrods (for mom and me) and "Phantom of the Opera" in Her Majesty's Theatre, every moment brought it's own thrill.

Not only was our trip educating and fun, but it was also filled with various opportunities to minister to the people of London. Our tour guide in the National History Museum was an ardent evolutionist who vivaciously portrayed the whole evolutionary process to us for around 3 hours. We just patiently listened to him and enjoyed God's creation. The museum was like none other that I've seen. It looked more like a huge, beautiful church. Actually its' arquitect Christopher Wrens, built the museum to bring honor to God—a kind of worship-causing place. Toward the end of our tour, including the back rooms of the architectural epitome filled with beakers and beakers of fish specimens preserved since the 1700's, he found out that we were missionaries and was astonished that we hadn't tried to "shout down" his evolutionary theories like other Christians he had met. He opened up to us, telling us why he had volunteered to give me the tour—because his mother had died of cancer. Inside, he was filled with bitterness against God and we were able to shed some of God's love on his life as well.

The Tower of London, an old battle castle, was also very fascinating. In there, we saw the Crown jewels and were awed by them. They really reminded me of heaven. There, the Yeomen Wardens all autographed and gave me a book about the jewels.

Before going to see the "Phantom of the Opera," mom and I were thoroughly spoiled in Harrod's spa with facials. I found it very relaxing; I even fell asleep during the process. From there, we got all dressed up for the evening of theater enjoyment. I had never been to an opera or play in my life, and found it very exciting.

On Sunday, we visited Holy Trinity Brompton Church and were blessed to be with our extended Christian family. We met many beautiful people and were encouraged in our faith as well.

We visited many places and had a memorable time in all, but even without the ritz and glamour we had a nice family time. We would go for lovely walks down Kensington Avenue, in the Kensington Park, and in little shops along the way. Many laughs and delights were shared. This trip was a victory one for us, too. Unlike a lot of other children who are granted wishes, I was blessed with health, strength, and renewed vigor on this dream-come-true, having finished all of my treatments and only being in the vigilance stage. Our family, who's always been close, just enjoyed our fellowship again. Yes, this dream will be one that we will never forget.

BALMORAL CASTLE

13th October, 2000

*Dear Arlene,*

I was so touched to receive your card after I met you and your family at Buckingham Palace back in September. It was a great joy to be able to speak to you as you really are an inspiration to others - you certainly inspired <u>me</u>!

And then I read the paper you sent me ... What you have been through, and endured with such courage, is beyond all belief, but is a shining testimony to your unshakeable faith in Our Lord and to the power of redemption. I have come to the conclusion during my life that we <u>all</u> have a cross to bear at some stage in our existence, but that "cross" comes in so many guises. It is suffering of some kind that brings us closer to God, I believe, and you, dear Arlene, have suffered more than most and are therefore closer to the Divine Source than most of us will ever be.

I have been reading a wonderful book recently about a truly remarkable and saint-like Russian monk who lived on Mount Athos in Greece. One of the extraordinary things he said he learnt from God during endless days of prayer, agony and contemplation was "to keep your mind in Hell - and <u>despair not</u>". You have never despaired and are a true example to us all. I am <u>sure</u> you are right and that the Good Lord has a definite purpose for you ...

This comes with many affectionate blessings and countless healing thoughts.

**Letter from Balmoral Palace**

**ST. JAMES'S PALACE**
**LONDON SW1A 1BS**

From:  The Assistant Private Secretary to HRH The Prince of Wales

22nd January 2001

*Dear Arlene,*

    The Prince of Wales has asked me to write to thank you for your lovely letter of New Year's Eve, and for the photographs you enclosed.

    His Royal Highness has asked me to say that he would certainly be ready to consider writing a foreword or message for your book.  Please send me a copy of the draft text, and I shall then put it to The Prince of Wales.  His Royal Highness added that he is perfectly happy for you to use your photograph taken with him.

    The Prince of Wales wanted you to know that the lamp is surviving well, despite the considerable use that it is having to endure!  This comes with His Royal Highness's warmest wishes, and many healing thoughts.

*with all good wishes,*

Nigel Baker

Miss Arlene Sheppard

**Letter from HRH Prince Charles, St. James Palace**

# Chapter 10

# "Come to Jesus and find...healing"

-------

"Well, even if we visit you with funny masks, you know we send hugs and love. Our family has shared some blood with you and we pray for a "Transfusion of Jesus' blood to boost and renew you."

"To the beautiful Sheppard family,

We heard the news of Arlene's temperature skyrocketing. We joined you in intercession. This morning, we were told that by 10:00 o'clock last night, it had returned to normal. A million Hallelujahs.

We continue to stand by you in prayer. We believe that Arlene has 'Health to her body and strength to her bones.' Because you (we) are trusting in the Lord with all your(our) heart, acknowledging Him in all your(our) ways. Because of your obedience to Him, He will direct your ways, showing you His will for Arlene and giving you the strength to walk through it with her. (Proverbs 3:5-8)

'As Jerusalem was met by the Lord in her affliction, so shall Arlene (Ezekiel 16:6).' And when I passed by you and saw you struggling in your own blood, I said to you in your blood, 'Live!; yes, I said to you in your blood, 'Live!' And God shall make Arlene to thrive, to grow and mature like a beautiful plant in the field. Love you lots!"

--------

When the cloud seems the darkest, that's when the Son shines the brightest. When you feel that you've reached your 'wit's end' and can't go on, that's when Jesus, the Bright Son, calls out to you, waiting for you to call out to Him.

"But to you who fear My name the Sun of Righteousness shall arise with healing in His wings:" (Malachi 4:2a, NKJV).

The Lord Jesus said, "Come unto me, all ye that labor and are heavy laden, and I will give thee rest" (Matt 11:28, KJV).

If someone were to ask me, "What did you learn from this experience? How can you actually be thankful that you went through leukemia?" It certainly was not easy and pain-free, but yet I learned to depend more on Jesus for my every need. Not only did He die on the cross for my sins, but also for my healing and wellness/wholeness (Shalom). We had to lean on our Father even more for the finances and for my healing. Sometimes, the Name of Jesus was the only whisper that could come out of my lips, but that more than sufficed. He was and is still the only Friend that I can truly ever rely on 100%. Throughout my treatments and still today, we call out to God for our needs. He's got good things for you, too!!

*"For I know the thoughts that I think toward you, says the Lord, thoughts of peace and not of evil, to give you a future and a hope"* (Jeremiah 29:1, NKJV).

*"But as it is written: 'Eye has not seen, nor ear heard, nor have entered into the heart of man the things which God has prepared for those who love Him"* (I Cor. 2:9, NKJV).

I would like to now share with you, the Reader, some of the verses from the Bible that really helped us.

### All who come to Jesus:

*"And Jesus went about all Galilee, teaching in their synagogues, preaching the gospel of the kingdom, and healing* **ALL** *kinds of sickness and* **ALL** *kinds of disease among the people. Then His fame went throughout all Syria; and they brought to Him all sick people who were afflicted with various disease and torments, and those who were demon-possessed, epileptics, and paralytics; and* **HE HEALED THEM***"* (Mtt.4:23-24, NKJV, **emphasis by the author**).

### Never stop praying!:

*"And the prayer of faith will save the sick, and the Lord will raise him up. And if he has committed sins, he will be forgiven. Confess your trespasses to one another, and pray for one another, that you may be healed. The effective, fervent prayer of a righteous man avails much"* (James 5:15-16, NKJV).

*"Beloved, I pray that you may prosper in all things and be in health, just as your soul prospers"* (III Jn. 2, NKJV).

### Jehovah Jireh, our provider:

*"And my God shall supply all your need according to His riches in glory by Christ Jesus"* (Phil. 4:19, NKJV).

*"And He said to me, "My grace is sufficient for you, for My strength is made perfect in weakness...For when I am weak, then I am strong"* (2 Cor. 12:9-10, NKJV).

*"Let us therefore come boldly to the throne of grace, that we may obtain mercy and find grace to help in time of need"* (Hebrews 4:16, NKJV).

### Jehovah Rapha, our healer:

*"and (He) said, 'If you diligently heed the voice of the Lord your God and do what is right in His sight, give ear to His commandments and keep all His statutes, I will put none of the diseases on you which I have brought on the Egyptians. For I am the Lord who heals you'"* (Ex. 15:26, NKJV). (Jesus is Yahweh, your personal physician!!)

*"Who Himself bore our sins in His own body on the tree, that we, having died to sins, might live for righteousness—by whose stripes you were healed"* (I Peter 2:24).

*"Surely He has borne our griefs and carried our sorrows; yet we esteemed Him stricken, smitten by God, and afflicted. But He was wounded for our transgressions, He was bruised for our iniquities; the chastisement for our peace was upon Him, and by His stripes we are healed"* (Isaiah 53:4-5).

*"Bless the Lord, O my soul; and all that is within me, bless His holy name! Bless the Lord, O my soul, and forget not all His benefits: Who forgives **ALL** your iniquities, Who heals **ALL** your disease, Who redeems your life from destruction, Who crowns you with lovingkindness and tender mercies, Who satisfies your mouth with good things, so that your youth is renewed like the eagle's"* (Psalm 103:1-5,NKJV, **emphasis by author**).

Chemotherapy, like I said earlier, is like a poison. Many parts of me could have been damaged, but I trust in the Lord who "renews" my life more and more into complete restoration!

### Jesus our ultimate Friend; I will not fear!:

*"I called on the Lord in distress; the Lord answered me and set me in a broad place. The Lord is on my side; I will not fear. **What can man do to me?** (Psalm 118: 5-6, NKJV)*

*"No temptation has overtaken you except such as is common to man; but **God is faithful**, who will not allow you to be tempted beyond what you are able, but with the temptation will also make the way of escape, that you may be able to bear it"* (I Cor. 10:13, NKJV, **emphasis by author**).

*"I sought the Lord, and He heard me, and delivered me from **ALL** my fears...The angel of the Lord encamps all around those who fear Him and delivers them"* (Psalm 34:4,7, NKJV, **emphasis by author**).

*"Be anxious for nothing, but in everything by prayer and supplication, with thanksgiving, let your requests be made known to God; and the **peace** of God, which surpasses all understanding, will guard your hearts and minds through Christ Jesus"* (Phil. 4:7, NKJV, **emphasis by author**).

*"The Lord is my helper; I will not fear. **What can man do to me?**** (Heb. 13:6, NKJV, **emphasis by author**).

### I will not die!!!

*"I shall not die, but **live**, and declare the works of the Lord"* (Psalm 118:17, NKJV).

*"The Lord is my strength and my song, and He has become my **salvation**; He is my God, and I will praise Him, My father's God, and I will exalt Him"* (Ex. 15:2, NKJV, **emphasis by author**).

### Jesus is always here for us.

*"...and lo, I am with you always, even to the end of the age"* (Mtt.28:20, NKJV).

*"Jesus Christ is the same yesterday, today, and forever"* (Heb. 13:8, NKJV).

## I will praise His Name forever!

*"Oh, give thanks to the Lord, for He is good! For His mercy endures forever"* (Psalm 118:29, NKJV).

*"The Lord has done great things for us, and we are glad"* (Psalm 126:3, NKJV).

Thank you so much for reading my book. I hope that you too, through having read this story or some other, will find the hope that I found. Find Jesus. **NEVER GIVE UP!**

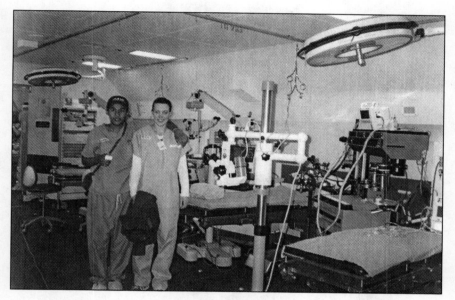

**Arlene translating on CBN Flying Hospital airplane**

**Arlene and Benji**

**Arlene teaching Children in Cuba**

**AJ and the founders of Make A Wish Foundation,**

# Epilogue

The Lord has brought me to new things in the last couple of years. For over two and a half years, now, I have been finished with all chemotherapy treatments! During this time, I also completed the two-year vigilance period, and now have a clean bill of health. My hair has grown back, too—it is now below my shoulders in length and curly! I graduated from high school over a year ago with honors and have been continuing my studies in music as well as teaching music classes. God has provided me with a good job that has allowed me to save up for the future. I received a full scholarship to Christ for the Nations, Dallas, Texas, to further my education.

I have a boyfriend now!! Benjamin is the best that there ever could be! The Lord brought us together at just the right time in my life. He's my first (and only) boyfriend and I am so grateful to the Lord for him. He tells me that I'm beautiful, and always whispers to me that he loves me. He makes me laugh and spoils me so—but most importantly, he also yearns to serve God with all of his heart, soul, and mind.

The great 'adventures' that I've been through continue to precede me in touching many lives. In September 2001, I went on a missionary trip to Cuba, visiting different villages and cities sharing what God has done in my life and praying for the sick. People here, in Puebla, Mexico call me up every now and then to pray for some loved one with cancer or to go and visit them. Because of what I've endured, I am able to go and do this with an understanding heart and the power of His healing Hand, knowing that my God heals the sick and broken-hearted. God has opened doors of ministry wherever we go—in Canada and in the USA as well. I pray that my life and testimony will continue to be used as long as I live. God is so good to me.

May 16, 2000

"This is the eighth book of my life. Wow. Praise the Lord for 17 years that He's given to me! It is only by Him that I am here and by Him I'll remain on this earth until He calls me home: "Daughter, it is time." Until that time comes, I will serve God with all my being and continue to grow in Him. Praise God!"

### *And the Story continues…*

It is now April 24, 2003, with plans of going to Christ for the Nations in a few months and getting married a few years down the road, I find myself struggling. I began to have migraine headaches a few months back which then was followed with extreme pain in my wrists and elbows, sometimes even in my knees. In my heart I know that I am healed, but my mind can play dirty tricks sometimes that cause uneasiness. I had this nose bleed a few weeks back that led us to take a blood test as I had grown quite weak and anemic. The blood test was very unnerving when it showed that 5 % of my blood had blastos or leukemia cells in it. The bone marrow test showed 98 % of leukemia. Here I was home-free from cancer for three years only to be bombarded with fears from the past. My heart cries out to God, my Saviour, "Oh, Lord why again?" I know that through the depths of despair He hears my cry. I know that I'm not going to die, but yet to pass through all the pain of the past again, seems impossible. To know what it is like makes the situation completely different. I know what the chemo can do to my body, I know what it's like to lose my hair, I know what it's like to have a puffy face, to have a port put under your skin….I know the nauseas and headaches and heartaches it can all cause…so why again? I believe that my God is going to give me a miracle instantaneously this time. He hasn't yet, but I know that He will. The past seems useless, having passed through three years of chemo only to be granted three more years of health, but yet I know that God has a purpose through all of this. I just want to get down to the light of hope at the end of the dark tunnel soon, Oh! So soon.

Three days ago, I was hospitalized to receive red blood cells and then to have a surgery to put a new port in, followed by chemo in my spine and by IV. Big day! My friends and my boyfriend went to keep me company and help the time pass faster. That was a huge help. Now, I've been recuperating, suffering from a very sore chest and throat from the surgery as well as nauseas sometimes. On Monday, I'm scheduled to start up chemo every day for the next two weeks. Right now, I am to reach remission. I look at all these grim circumstances with dread, but I know that my God's grace will be sufficient for me, His strength is made perfect in my weakness.

*********************

Note: Several months passed before we, her parents had the strength to look for her book manuscript and we found the epilogue she had written as you've just read it.

*********************

*God's grace was sufficient for Arlene, as well as for the rest of her family and friends. Between two and three o'clock pm June 25, 2003 "heaven's gates opened" and Arlene was welcomed into the loving arms of her Lord and Savior. She, her family and hundreds of other friends prayed and believed for a miracle, but our idea of a miracle never happened. Instead, God, knowing the true desires of her heart, in His sovereignty chose to take her to himself. All of the days ordained for her were written in His book.(Psalm 139:16)*

*Arlene is now where we all desire to be someday, and has joined the "faithful cloud of witnesses" up above, cheering us on, as we finish the race God has called us to. We miss her intensely, but know that her life will live on through this book and through the many lives impacted by her short one. We trust, precious reader, that this book has given you a greater compassion for the sick and suffering and their families. May it also have given hope to those of you whose prayers were not answered in the way you expected, and your loved ones went home early. Those who put their trust in the Lord Jesus can never lose. Whether we live a long or short time on this earth, we will all be together for eternity with the Lord.*

*Her parents, David & Rowene Sheppard*
*©2007*

<u>A Little Prayer of Arlene's, probably written after her relapse in 2003:</u>

*Oh God, You are my God and I will ever praise you! God, take me into Your loving arms and may I fly with you over all my problems and pain... heal me, restore me, transform my life... Make me whole again, Restore to me the joy of my salvation and renew a right spirit within me, Hug me, hold me, help me to keep on keeping on. For You are great and greatly to be praised! I want to cry into your shoulders, have you wipe my tears.*

---------------------------------------------------------

<u>More recently, in June 2005,</u> our family was in Zacatlan, Puebla, in central Mexico and there we met a young pastor from Canada who had a very interesting story we want to share with you. Here's his story.

I was at a pastor's prayer meeting in Abbotsford, BC, when a prayer request was given for a young girl. She was the daughter of missionaries in Mexico and she was dying of leukemia. We were asked to pray for her complete healing. As we all entered into prayer, some of the pastors were praying for her healing when I went into a vision. I saw the most beautiful young lady that looked like she was in her late teens or so. She was so beautiful with her long brown hair. As she was looking to the heavens with her arms outstretched, such an unimaginable peace, joy, and love was literally glowing from her face. It was as if she had complete and total freedom for the first time in her life! Then I saw Jesus looking to her from the heavens with the most beautiful expression of joy on His face. It was as if He had been waiting for her for so long to be with Him like a groom that sees his bride coming to him! As they drew close, His arms were outstretched for His true love to come. I saw tears of unexplainable joy running down both of there faces, and the tears fell back to the earth. It was as if each tear had a purpose to give joy into the lives they touched, and the tears spread all over Mexico, North America, and beyond. Almost as if her story would be told and many lives would be changed through her and Christ's love.

I immediately knew that I could not pray for her physical healing as God was calling her home to be with him, and she nor Jesus wanted me to interfere.

This experience was so intense that I had to leave the meeting immediately and could not come back that day. A few days later I had heard that she had passed away, and my heart leaped with such joy as I knew she was dancing with her groom in the heavens! I told my wife that even though I do not know the missionaries names, but one day I hoped to meet her parents because I knew that I needed to tell them what I saw.

This experience radically helped me understand more about God's sovereignty and healing, as I have used this testimony while preaching in many countries of the world since. Little did I know that during one of our crusades in Zacatlan Mexico, July 2005, I would start praying for a husband and wife that were missionaries in Mexico. To my amazement, but God's divine plan, it was David and Rowene Sheppard, the parents of the young lady, Arlene. As I was now praying with the parents, I immediately went into another vision and I saw the young girl Arlene with my mom Vera Borthwick who passed away in 1989 after being missionaries for 50 years, dancing together in the courts of heaven. Immediately Arlene said to her parents "I love you so much, and you will always be my mommy and daddy. I will see you soon."

Obviously we were all crying together as we felt an incredible well of joy! David pulled out a picture of Arlene and it was exactly the girl that I saw!

"Arlene, I know that we have never met in the physical, but I want to thank you for all that you have done and are still doing on this earth. Thank you for the great joy that many of us have experienced from you, and for the many more that will see the love of Jesus as your ministry carries on."

Love in the name of your groom Jesus Christ,

Brent Borthwick
President/Founder
Wind Word Ministries
www.windword.ca

*****************

Here we want to include several poems written by her friends.

### Arlene Joy

On June 25 God looked down
And where He looked Arlene was found
He opened up His loving arms
And welcomed her into His Kingdom afar
Her suffering was ended and replaced with peace
As her beautiful soul went off to meet
Meet the Lord in the sky, high above
And feel the warmth of Jesus' love
The angels sang, all Heaven rejoiced
The Pearly Gates opened and the trumpets were voiced
We'll never forget the joys she brought
Or her lovely smile and positive thoughts
The wonderful person we all knew and loved
Is now with our Lord Jesus in Heaven above

Love,
Lise
(© Lise Malta is a cousin of Arlene)

## Her Name Was Joy

Sent from the Father, on loan for a time,
Her mission known only to Him,
A daughter was born to a family on earth,
Her future entrusted to them.
    And they named her Arlene Joy.

Her parents, good stewards of this precious gift,
Taught her to serve and to love.
Her happy, sweet nature, her radiant smile,
Were signs of a peace from above.
    And she brought them lots of Joy.

Her gifts from the Father were received with grace,
Her music, a blessing to share.
She ministered healing and comfort and cheer,
To those heavy-laden with care.
    As they listened to the Joy.

Her love for the Father could always be seen,
Her faith, an example to all.
She only desired to bring glory to Him,
And be sensitive unto His call.
    And her heart was full of Joy.

In times of her suffering, she still had a song
That came from down deep in her heart.
Her Heavenly Father gave mercy and peace
And assurance they never would part.
    And His presence gave her Joy.

Her time here on earth seemed so short to us all,
And we didn't want her to go.
But she heard the voice of her Father so dear,
"My daughter, it's time to come home.
    And enter into my great JOY."

© 2003 Kathryn Owen Gray

## <u>She Graced Us</u>

*She Graced Us with a smile - from the very beginning.*
*Never faltering was her Joy in Him.*

*She Graced Us with music from heaven, touching our hearts*
*with a beauty only He could bestow.*

*She Graced Us with love for everyone she crossed paths with, and*
*especially the ones she walked with side-by-side.*

*She Graced Us with strength that none of us could have possessed,*
*Showing all of us what strength in Him could do.*

*She Graced Us with words - so special - Oh! What a gift given by*
*Him above to bless so many others.*

*She Graced Us with Joy - always spreading her namesake*
*no matter her pain, or sorrow.*

*She Graced Us with life - never faltering - never weakening – the life*
*inside was stronger than her body*

*She Graced Us - Yes she did.*

*Arlene Joy - We will miss your love, your joy, and your life.*
*We'll see you again at His Glorious Appearing!*
*We love you now, and forever!*

(©written by Nichole Dicken, a dear friend from Texas (7/12/03)

Jerry and Vicky Love mexmish@pacto.org
Dearest David, Rowene and Michael,

Your—our—beautiful Arlene, gifted by the loveliest of graces, always wanted to meet royalty. Here she was once granted the opportunity to be in the presences of a potentate. But today, she was received by The KING. And when He held out His hand to her, she realized that she was His eternal princess.

### Finally Home

**"But just think…..of stepping on shore, and finding it's heaven!**
   **….of touching a hand, and finding it's God's.**
      **…..of breathing anew air, and finding it's celestial**
   **—mmmm-mmmmm**
      **……of waking up in glory, and finding you are home.**

When surrounded by the blackness of the darkest night,
   Oh how lonely death could be.
      But at the end of this dark tunnel is a shining light and
         Death is swallowed up in victory.

**But just think……of stepping on the shore, and finding it's heaven!**
   **….of touching a hand, and finding it's God's.**
      **…..of breathing anew air, and finding it's celestial**
   **—mmmm-mmmmm**
      **……of waking up in glory, and finding you are home.**

Vicky Love

If you have any questions or need a friend, please write:
David and Rowene Sheppard, E-Mail: d.sheppard@mail.com

**<u>The End</u>**

Printed in the United States
105434LV00006B/25-114/A